D1604037

Advance Praise for

RADICAL LOVING

"*Radical Loving* is a gem! It is not just a book about love—it is a book written from love. It is a prose-poem to God and to all of us; a tapestry that weaves together all spiritual traditions to celebrate the oneness of God, of our world, and of all people. With tales, parables, anecdotes, recollections, keen insights, and wisdom teachings, Rabbi Dosick gives us the profound vision of a spiritual awakening that speaks directly to the heart of every reader and gives us hope." —Rabbi David Zaslow, author, *Jesus: First Century Rabbi*, and *Reimagining Exodus*

"This beautifully written call to love is more than an invitation; it is a lantern in the night. Rabbi Wayne Dosick lives the wisdom he offers us here. I have rarely met a person with such consistent generosity of spirit, willing to take the risk of loving at all costs, as this gentle master of the human heart. This book reminds us that we belong to each other—all of us—and that this belonging is our salvation." —Mirabai Starr, author, *God of Love: A Guide to the Heart of Judaism, Christianity, and Islam*, and *Wild Mercy: Living the Fierce and Tender Wisdom of the Women Mystics*

"Don't be fooled by Rabbi Dosick's deceptively simple writing! His beautiful prose is lilting and playful, but his message is radical and deep. Beware: if taken to heart, this is a book that will change your life!" —Rabbi Tirzah Firestone, Ph.D., author, *Wounds into Wisdom*

"Rabbi Wayne Dosick, deeply grounded in sacred literature, offers profound insights in a manner accessible to people of all backgrounds. *Radical Loving* is a veritable GPS to an expanded inner life. Drawing on the wisdom of traditions of the past, this rabbi-sage applies them forcefully to the challenges of the present, and illuminates the path to a just and peaceful future. This is a compendium of spiritual knowledge that the reader will return to many times for inspiration and guidance." —Rabbi Leah Novick, author, *On the Wings of Shekhinah: Rediscovering Judaism's Divine Feminine*

"Reading *Radical Loving* reminds me of who I Am at my best! It gives me great hope, and it inspires me to want to do good, to want to be a better person." —Annie Klein, Certified Sage-ing Leader

"I am honored that my soul-brother, Rabbi Wayne Dosick, chronicles our spiritual friendship in this extraordinary book, *Radical Loving*. I pray that millions of people around the world will be inspired by the good rabbi's wise and wonderful teachings, and come to understand that we are all children of the One God, and that our collective fate and future depends on embracing each other in unity and love. In the Name of God and all that is holy, please read this book!" —The Rev. Fr. James J. O'Leary, S. J., Spiritual Director, Marquette University

"In fractious times in a fractured world, Rabbi Wayne Dosick's book arrives as a much needed healing balm and a call to remember the essential truth at the foundation of life—we are one. Through poetic writing, rich spiritual insights, uplifting quotations and stories that awaken and illumine, our experiences of contemporary life are balanced and transformed. We are elevated above the fray and set on the higher ground of living with love, openness, compassion and caring. I am a better person for reading this book!" —Rev. Dr. Kathy Hearn, Dean, The School of Spiritual Leadership, Encinitas, CA; former national president, Centers for Spiritual Living

"In the hell of Auschwitz, even at the tender age of fifteen, I decided that I would not be a victim, but, rather, a triumphant survivor. What was around me did not matter anywhere near as much as what was inside me, so I fully covered myself in love. Now, this precious child of spirit, Rabbi Wayne Dosick, offers this same prescription to our troubled world. Do not separate yourself from the human family. Do not hate. Love. Love. Love. Please read this wise and inspiring book right now, and love, love, love with all your heart." —Dr. Edith Eva Eger, author, *The Choice: Embrace the Possible*

"Our precious children have come to Earth to be the paradigm-shifters who lead us to a more perfect world. Rabbi Wayne Dosick's *Radical Loving* is the visionary and inspiring book that guides our children and us to grasp hands and hearts in dynamic love to bring peace and harmony to our planet." —Jan Tober and Dr. Lee Carroll, World Teachers and authors of *The Indigo Children: The New Kids Have Arrived*, and the Kryon series

"With *Radical Loving*, Rabbi Wayne Dosick joins the ranks of great thinkers and feelers who, with the audacity of radical *chutzpah*, offers a recipe for fixing the world. It arrives just in time. Our fractured, coarsened, and depleted planet is in desperate need of the unification and relief that can only come from reclaimed love. A fusion of theology, manifesto, and spiritual memoir, packaged within the poetry of an entertaining read, this is a book that may change minds and will most certainly touch the heart." —Thane Rosenbaum, author, *How Sweet It Is!*, *The Golems of Gotham*, *Second Hand Smoke*, and *Elijah Visible*

"*Radical Loving* by our dear spiritual elder Rabbi Wayne Dosick comes at the right time in our lives. Dedicated to my teacher and mentor Elie Wiesel, of blessed memory, it helps bring us to a holy place where we can try to bring more light into our fractured world. Elie Wiesel taught us that we should try to see more humanity in each other's eyes. This book helps us to see more clearly through a lens of love and compassion." —Cantor Deborah Katchko-Gray, Founder, The Women Cantor's Network; author, *Katchko: Three Generations of Cantorial Art*

"In *Radical Loving: One God. One World. One People*, Rabbi Wayne Dosick shares from a deep wellspring of Jewish tradition, life-experience, and personal questing. This book is a kaleidoscope of musings and deep teachings, and a weave of bringing knowledge from a multiple of sources into a wholeness that will astound and delight the reader. Through his sharing and questioning, we as readers, are invited to reflect on our own individual path. The result is a book that is very personal and, at the same time, trans-personal, and sorely needed throughout the whole world at this pivotal time." —Rabbi Lynn Claire Feinberg, Chief Liberal Rabbi of Norway

"There is no other book like *Radical Loving*. It is written in one, long, holy breath. It is a teaching about love. A plea and a prayer for unity and peace. It is like a wedding ceremony between humans and the Divine. It is a poem about life and the beauty of the human heart. It is an invitation to give, serve, bond, honor, laugh, forgive, listen, learn, and enjoy the smorgasbord of the created universe. Rabbi Dosick is a prophet for modern times, and his prophecy is a four-letter word: love." —Judith Fein, author, *How to Communicate with the Dead*, *Life is a Trip*, and *The Spoon from Minkowitz*

"Rabbi Wayne Dosick asks the oldest but most urgent questions and recasts our oldest wisdom to speak answers to today. We need radical loving to make the crises we are living through now bearable." —Rodger Kamenetz, author of *The Jew in the Lotus* and *The History of Last Night's Dream*

"In the Vedic tradition of Sanatan Dharma everything in creation is One. Namaste is the Sanskrit word expressing that. Through his writing, Rabbi Wayne Dosick eloquently awakens this feeling and understanding. Every cell in the body can become more enlivened with Divine energy by reading *Radical Loving*. Many parts brought tears to my eyes to hear these truths so beautifully expressed. I appreciate this sage Rabbi because he went into deepness to bring this message out, and writes these kind of thoughts. He knows how Lord made this world. And he gives practical ways to learn and embody what it means to be a good human being. We can all be inspired by the power of these words. Namaste." —Pandit Shiv Mohan Trivedi, Maharishi Vedic Pandit, Agra, India

"*Radical Loving* is a song from the heart of creation, written in an inspired and inspiring language that awakens the reader. Dedicated to Elie Wiesel, this book elaborates on his commitments to humanity, to storytelling, and to hope. Rabbi Dr. Wayne Dosick offers profound teachings and tales to remind us that we are not alone, that we can create new realities, and that our human future depends on reclaiming the intangible, the ineffable: love." —Rabbi Ariel Burger, Ph.D., author *Witness: Lessons From Elie Wiesel's Classroom*

"Rabbi Dosick has written more theological books than this one, but none wiser or more courageous. While his idiom here is Jewish, my liberal Catholic heart is cheering." —Jon M. Sweeney, co-author of *Meister Eckhart's Book of the Heart*

RADICAL

LOVING

ONE GOD

ONE WORLD

ONE PEOPLE

Rabbi Wayne Dosick, PhD

Monkfish Book Publishing Company
Rhinebeck, New York

Grateful acknowledgment to:
Jonah and Rebecca Balogh for use of their Lineage Process.
The heirs of Ruth F. Brin *zt"l* for her poem "For the Blessings," a.k.a. "Illuminations."
The Estate of Rabbi Shlomo Carlebach *zt"l* for the words to "*U'vene Yerushalayim*" and "Return Again." For more information: NeshamaCarlebach@gmail.com.

Hardcover ISBN 978-1-948626-27-9
eBook ISBN 978-1-948626-28-6

Library of Congress Cataloging-in-Publication Data

Names: Dosick, Wayne D., 1947- author.
Title: Radical loving : one God, one world, one people / Rabbi Wayne Dosick, PhD.
Description: Rhinebeck, New York : Monkfish Book Publishing Company, 2021. | Includes bibliographical references.
Identifiers: LCCN 2020050719 (print) | LCCN 2020050720 (ebook) | ISBN 9781948626279 (hardcover) | ISBN 9781948626286 (ebook)
Subjects: LCSH: Love--Religious aspects. | Social history--21st century. | Good and evil--Religious aspects.
Classification: LCC BL626.4 .D67 2021 (print) | LCC BL626.4 (ebook) | DDC 205/.677--dc23
LC record available at https://lccn.loc.gov/2020050719
LC ebook record available at https://lccn.loc.gov/2020050720

Front cover design by Glen Edelstein
Book design by Colin Rolfe
Author photo by Mark Lewis Glickman

Monkfish Book Publishing Company
22 East Market Street, Suite 304
Rhinebeck, NY 12572
(845) 876-4861
monkfishpublishing.com

To
the Holy Memory
of

ELIE WIESEL *zt"l*

witness of the destruction
teller of the tale
restorer of the broken
conscience of the generation
voice of the silent
Laureate of Peace

Let there be love between us.
Let us return to what we learned in Heaven before we were born.

Seeing your face is like seeing the Face of God.

The only way to get it together is together.

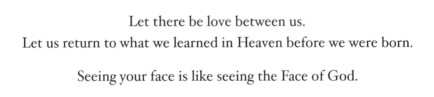

— *Rabbi Shlomo Carlebach zt"l*
—*Genesis 33:10*
— *Rabbi Zalman Schachter-Shalomi zt"l*

CONTENTS

THE FIRST WORD

What an incredible time it is to be alive!

What a privilege it is to be in a body on Earth at this moment!

We live in the magnificence of Earth's stunning beauty.

We are the crown of creation.

We are partners in the ongoing unfolding of the universe.

We stand at yet another pinnacle of scientific, medical, and technological exploration.

We hold the design for goodness and righteousness, equality, justice, decency, dignity, grace, kindness, compassion, and love.

We constantly evolve human consciousness and reveal more and more of the mysteries of the universe.

We embody unleashed growth and unlimited potential.

We are God's precious children, living on God's glorious Earth, bathed in the Light of God's splendor.

How fortunate are we!

How sweet and good our lives can be!

And yet ...

OF THEN AND NOW

An old, old story.[1]
Of Then and Now.

Then.

A long, long time ago in a faraway place, there was a small village. On one side of the village was a great ocean, and on the other side were high mountains.

A few of the people in the village made their living by fishing, but most of the men and women and children worked in the rice fields that were high on top of one of the mountains.

Every morning, the villagers climbed the mountain path to work in the fields. Every evening, they trekked down the mountains to sleep in the village huts.

Only a grandmother—and her granddaughter whose name was Hanako—lived on top of the mountain, where it was their job to keep the fires lit at night to scare off the wild animals who might eat the rice.

Early one morning during the season when the rice fields turned golden dry, ready for the harvest, Grandmother tended the fire. Down below, the villagers began their morning chores before climbing the mountain to begin the day's work.

As she did every morning after first stirring the fire, Grandmother went to the mountain's edge to watch the sun rise. But, on this day, she did not see the sun coming up. Instead, what she saw brought terrible fear.

As quickly as she could, she ran to the hut where her granddaughter was sleeping. "Hanako," she called, "Get up. Get up!"

"Oh, Grandmother," said Hanako, "I am tired. Please let me sleep."

"No, my child. Get up right now and do as I say. Get a burning stick from the fire."

Hanako knew that she must do as she was told, for she had never heard her grandmother so frightened. Hanako went to get a burning stick from the fire and, soon, she joined her grandmother who was standing out in the field.

Grandmother cried out a command: "Burn the rice fields!"

"But, Grandmother," Hanako cried, "we cannot burn the rice fields. This is our village's food. Without this rice, we will all starve."

"Do as I say," commanded Grandmother.

With tears streaming down her face, Hanako did as she was told. She touched the burning stick to the fields and set the precious rice on fire. Soon, large clouds of smoke rose up from the rice fields on the top of the mountain.

Down below, the villagers saw the smoke, and in moments every man, woman, and child in the village came running up the mountain.

When they reached the top, they could see the flames destroying their precious rice. Their whole crop was ruined.

"What happened here?" they cried out. "How did this horrible fire begin?"

"I set the fire," Grandmother told the villagers.

"What? You set the fire? You stupid old woman! You have ruined our rice crop. We will all starve. How could you do such a horrible thing?"

"Come with me," said Grandmother as she walked toward the edge of the mountain. "Look," she said as she pointed out toward the sea. "Look at that great storm that is bringing enormous waves coming toward the shore. In less than an hour, a wall of water will hit our little village, and everything will be destroyed."

The people stood quietly watching, and before long they saw that Grandmother was absolutely right. The heaving ocean brought huge waves onto the shore, and every hut in the village was crushed under a deluge of water.

The villagers looked down at their little village, which lay in waste, and they looked at the rice fields that were burned down, and one man cried out, "We have nothing left. Everything is gone. We are ruined."

And every villager wept and mourned.

But one woman said, "All is not lost. When we saw the smoke signal from the fire Grandmother set, we ran up here to the top of the mountain. We may not have our rice, but we have our lives. Every one of us has survived the great flood."

"That is right, my children," said a village Elder. "We have our lives. So, this afternoon we will start all over again. We will build new huts and plant new fields."

And for the rest of her days, Grandmother was honored and revered for her wisdom and her courage.

Now.

It seems to many that our world is being overtaken by great storms, and that we are all about to drown. The heaviness of hatred, and division, and violence, and terror, and war, and greed, and political folly of the present moment burdens our spirits and threatens the soul of all humanity.

Human and civil rights and liberties are being trampled; the powerless and the poor are being exploited while the elite and the wealthy become more powerful; diversity and equality are squashed; uninformed biases rage.

Refugees still wander; the hungry go unfed; addictions are rampant; the voices of minorities are being muted; the free press is being intimidated; danger lurks around every corner; fear grips.

In our bewilderment and our angst, we wonder—we cry out: How long must the world suffer in strife before brave hearts and determined hands pull us back from the nonsense of this madness?

Temporal solutions and the political expediencies of the moment offer little.

Not then.

Not now.

In this highly technological age—where the vast world has become a tiny village—there will be no losers or winners.

We need to learn to live together lest we perish together.

There is but one pathway. It is a pathway that requires great and resolute courage.

We've known about it, we've lived with it, since the moment of creation.

It comes to us from the eternal wisdom and the universal truths
    that are within each of us.

Sometimes we forget; sometimes we choose to ignore.

But the stakes are too high; the time is too fleeting.

Who are we?

How shall we live?

How shall we be?

The answer is right before us.

We must Re-Member.

The answer will gladden and ennoble us.

The answer will save us.

    The village and the field can rise up again
    And the villagers can forever tell the tale.

NAMING IT

Age-old wisdom teaches, "You do not know something until you know its name."

When we name the sickness, the poison that oozes throughout our world, we can begin to fight it and defeat it.

We see the evil: discordant division because of race, religion, ethnicity, gender, or class—the demonizing of "The Other."

We see the evil: the rise of xenophobia, radical Islamic fundamentalism, racism, racial profiling, white nationalism, white supremacists, the Ku Klux Klan, neo-Nazis, neo-fascists, anti-Semitism, Islamophobia, sexism, misogyny, ethnic discrimination, apartheid, bigotry, senseless hatred, brutal violence, terrorism, and the despoiling of our planet.

We see the evil: so-called "charismatic" men and women who rise up to play on the vulnerabilities and the emotions of the people; they separate, divide, and create fear by pitting one group against another, and ultimately crush hope by wreaking havoc on their own country and the world.

We remember: the hatred, bigotry, and discrimination of not-too-distant days that still ripple toward us; the footsteps of war and destruction; the horrors of the machines of genocide that still ripple through the lands. The words of young Anne Frank—hidden away when she was caught up in the madman's evil darkness—echo through the years, "I hear the approaching thunder that, one day, will destroy us."

There is no nice way to say this. These are pure evils—a defilement of all that is good and decent. The perpetrators violate the precepts and principles of human values and virtues and set themselves apart from our civilized society.

There are not two sides to evil or good people on both sides of evil. There are no excuses, justifications, or rationalizations for evil.

Those who ignore or dismiss evil do so only from their own ignorance and prejudice—for their own power, pleasure, or profit.

Evil in our world must be eradicated and left in the garbage heap of history.

The Good News is that men and women of peace and good will can rise up against evil, for we understand the words of the modern genius-visionary Albert Einstein, who famously remarked, "The world will not be destroyed by those who do evil, but by those who watch them without doing anything."

We cannot let evil triumph.

We can act now before it is too late.

We have a world to save.

This simple little book can be our guide.

The sacred journey toward healing and transformation now begins.

Come on the Journey.

Join in the Quest.

ON THIS JOURNEY

We all know that our fractured country and fractious world cannot be addressed by politics as usual or by the sweet sentiments of friendship or love that greeting cards and popular songs so often depict. There must be sweeping, fundamental, universal transformation.

The issues raised here will be very familiar to you. You may very well say to yourself: So what? Who cares? I already know all the problems he is raising, and I either already passionately agree or vehemently disagree with the solutions he is offering. And besides, his ideas have very little chance of being implemented and less chance of having any real impact or success.

Yes.

And—

We cannot sit idly by, hoping that time and an eventual return to good sense and congeniality will wipe away what is shattering us and our world. We need to be clear and stark in naming what is at stake and in acknowledging the urgency with which we must act.

My hope is that these words that are spoken from my heart and soul will infuse your thoughts and feelings—resonating in already open hearts and helping to soften hardened hearts; that—out of echoing and retelling—new awareness, understanding, energy, and urgency will bubble up into every fiber of your being.

While I respect and honor every religion and faith community's pathway, since my own background is Judaism, many of the sources, references, and allusions will be from the Jewish tradition. I hope that you will easily transfer my attributions into your own idiom so that you can more comfortably embrace the spirit and the meaning of this transmission.

The raw (and inconvenient) truth for me: Since I am passionately Jewish, this is a very hard book for me to write because, in many instances, I may be advocating against my own personal, ethnic, religious, cultural, and social special interests. Yet that is exactly why I must write: to bring the message that we all—every one of us—must rise above our own selfish needs and strive for the common good, the greater good. I am leaving many of my long-held, comfortable beliefs and behaviors and venturing into the unknown. And I am asking you to do the same. For we know that the current condition of our world is bringing too much conflict and pain to too many and that there must be a better way to live together for the betterment and well-being of all.

And, in this book, is God. "Bidden or unbidden, God always is present."[1]

My compass and guidepost have always been the word of God. I am its student, and I am its teacher. It is my life and the length of my days.

We talk to God. God listens. And then, God comes to us in words, and visions, and day and night dreams. And we really have to listen and see—to be open, clear channels; to be empty enough for God to come through us.

I ask you to listen. And to see. And to understand. And then to give your heart and your hands to responding.

These incredible challenging times call us to nothing less than a radical shift in human consciousness, a sweeping revolution, an unbounded evolution and transformation of humankind and the planet we inhabit. We envision a complete, unconditional, unreserved embrace of the World of Spirit and a World of Oneness.

Can we heal our broken world? Can we wipe away the darkness and bring the light? Can we see the face of love in every human being? Can we jubilantly embrace the pathway that will lead us forward to Eden on Earth?

Please.

Let's try.

> There are those who look at things the way they are,
> and ask "Why?"
> I dream of things that never were, and ask
> "Why not?"[2]

IN THE VERY, VERY BEGINNING

An old, old legend.

In the beginning, God created:

- ⚬ light and darkness—day and night;
- ⚬ the Heavens;
- ⚬ the seas, and the Earth-land;
- ⚬ the grass, and seeds, and trees;
- ⚬ the sun, moon, and stars;
- ⚬ fish and fowl; and the creeping, crawling insects of the land.[1]

And there was evening, and there was morning, a fifth day. And the Angels said to God, "Congratulations! You have created a magnificent universe. It is beautiful. Your new Earth will be a perfect reflection of our place here in Your Upper Abode. Well done, God. Well done" (adaptation Gen. Rabbah 8:5).

And God said, "Thank you very much, My dear Angels. But I am not yet finished creating. There is still more to do."

The Angels asked, "What do You mean?"

God said, "I have created the physical place and the creatures of the Earth who will live in that place—the fish, the birds, the bugs. But My creation is not complete. Tomorrow, on the sixth day, I will create the animals of the field. And then I will make human beings—man and woman—who will be the crowning work of creation. They will grow and grow in numbers so that their descendants will inhabit the land. And they will be My image on Earth. I will love them, and they will love Me. And they will love each other."

The Angels held their collective breath, for they were dumb-founded. There was absolute silence in the Heavenly Abode. "What's wrong?" asked God. "Why are you not thrilled and excited about what I will create tomorrow?"

Now, it is not easy to contradict or—*gasp!*—oppose God. Yet finally, with great courage and more than a bit of concern about the possible repercussions, the Head Angel—the one who was God's most trusted advisor—spoke up. The Angel said, "God, please, please do not do it. I know that I speak for all the Angels when I tell You that creating human beings will be a most grievous error."

God was amazed. "Why shouldn't I create the animals? They will be My perfect land-companions. And why shouldn't I create man and woman? They will be most like Me on Earth. They will do My will; they will become My co-creative partners with Me in enriching the Earth; and they will bring honor to My Name."

And the Head Angel said, "With all due respect, our dear, most-revered God, it will be exactly the opposite. Your human beings will destroy the magnificence of Your creation. They will trample the plants and the grasses of Your beautiful Earth; they will cut down the trees and leave Your forests bare. They will rape Your land of its precious gems and minerals. They will sully Your skies, and Your rivers, and Your oceans with their pollution and their waste.

"You will give them a brilliant code of behavior, telling them how to love You and one another; how to treat each other with decency and dignity; how to embrace and celebrate the Oneness of the human family.

"But they will forget—or worse, ignore—Your message of goodness. They will violate Your ethical injunctions. In their perversion, they will become wayward and wanton. In their greed, they will battle for power and control. They will soon pay no heed to Your call to kind-ness and compassion, goodness and righteousness. They will shatter the harmony of Your Divine Design. One will try to dominate the other, and instead of loving, they will begin to hate. And they will struggle, and attack, and eventually wage war with the other. And—most tragically—they will maim and kill each other.

"Please God, please do not do it. Please do not create human beings. All they will do is ruin Your glorious creation. All they will do is bring You disappointment and pain. They will break Your heart, and for eternity You will regret creating them."

God said, "Thank you for your wise counsel. I Am very touched by your concern. Actually, I can't help but wonder if you are, perhaps, not a bit jealous, for when I create human beings, you, My sweet Angels, will no longer be My only helpmates. But even if your motives are entirely pure and you really have only My highest good at heart, I Am not convinced by your arguments. Tomorrow, as soon as the new sun begins to rise east of Eden, I Am going to create the animals, and then man and woman."

"Why, God, why?" asked the Head Angel. "Why will you create these beings who can cause you so much trouble and anguish?"

And God said, "It is simple. My creation on the Earth below is perfect. It is stunningly magnificent. But you, my Heavenly Angels, will not be with Me there. Without human beings, Earth will be just another pretty place in the great panoply of My universes. When I Am there, without human beings I will not have any companions. I will not have any to talk with, or to play with, or to co-create with. On the grand new Earth, without men and women I will be lonely."

So, not wanting to be alone, not wanting to be without companionship on Earth, God created man and woman.

And there was evening, and there was morning, a sixth day.

And on the seventh day, God ceased from the work of creation and rested.

THEN WHAT HAPPENED?

And then?

Then there was Oneness on Earth. Oneness was known as Paradise. It was called the Garden of Eden, where all lived in harmony with one another.

Originally, there was one very special Tree in the heart of the Garden. This One Tree was actually two trees entwined and braided together—the Tree of Life, and the Tree of Knowledge of Good and Evil. This One Tree held the Oneness, the wholeness, of the new Earth.

The first human beings—let's call them Adam and Eve—were told:

> *"Of every tree of the Garden you are free to eat, but as for the Tree of Knowledge of Good and Evil, you must not eat of it. For as soon as you eat of it, you shall surely die."*
>
> *When the woman saw that the Tree was good for eating and a delight to the eyes, she took of its fruit and ate it. She also gave some to her husband, and he ate.*
>
> *And the Lord God said, "Now that man has become like one of us, knowing good and evil, what if he should stretch out his hand and take also from the Tree of Life and eat, and live forever?" So the Lord God banished him from the Garden of Eden.*[1]

Adam and Eve violated the instruction. They ate from the Tree of Knowledge of Good and Evil, humankind was expelled from the Garden, and the one entwined tree split into two. The Tree of Life—carrying the Divine Masculine energy—remained standing upright. The Tree of Knowledge of Good and Evil—carrying the Divine Feminine energy—was turned upside down and buried in the Earth.

Feminine Consciousness and wisdom went underground for eons and eons.[2]

With the perfection of Oneness broken, Earth fell from the higher Consciousness of Oneness (which some call the Fifth Dimension) to a denser Consciousness—the Third-Dimension world in which we now live. In this denser Consciousness, Oneness, shatters. SEPARATION is possible.

Humankind lost its perfect alignment with the Divine and was exiled from the Garden Paradise, sent to wander far from the Oneness of the Source of Creation. The Earth and her inhabitants began to experience the pangs and the pain of the separation.

It was not long after the Fall that our foibles and flaws, failings and faithlessness, began to fill the Earth. Our early stories that set the pattern of life on Earth are filled with jealousies, antagonisms, corruption, debauchery, and murder.

Consider: Cain and Abel, the Tower of Babel, the Flood, Sodom and Gomorrah, the banishment of the firstborn, the knife hovering over the throat of the beloved son, and the agony of empty wombs; schemers and tricksters, deceivers and scammers; conning of the father; the collusion of the mother; brothers turned against brothers, devastated families, and broken dreams. The early history of our spiritual ancestors became imprinted on our genes and has played out generation after generation, even to this very day. Our deepest archetypal myths express our reality.

With the Fall, the Divine Feminine—which we call SHECHINAH, the indwelling, nurturing, feminine aspect of the Divine—was horribly upset. Humankind's exile from the Garden broke Her heart.

In Her pain, Shechinah vowed to accompany humankind into exile so that, in our separation, we would at least be able to still have contact with the Divine. So She separated Herself from the Divine Masculine so that humankind could always find Her and not feel the pangs of loneliness. Thus, the wholeness, the totality, of God was broken too.

When we lost Paradise, we lost Oneness. We have been in spiritual exile ever since. The exile mentality, the pain and disconnection of separation, has shaped the course of human history and *Herstory* ever since.

Can we end the exile?

Can we return to the Garden of Oneness?

Can we make the Tree of Life and the Tree of the Knowledge of Good and Evil One—straight, and whole again?

AND NOW?

The kindergarten teacher told her students that
they could take a piece of paper and their crayons
and make a picture of anything they wanted to draw.
After a little while, the teacher walked around the classroom
to see what the students were drawing.
Will was making a picture of a house.
Claire was drawing a picture of her family.
Anna was coloring a beautiful rainbow.
When the teacher came to Jennifer,
it wasn't quite clear what Jennifer was drawing.
So the teacher said, "Jennifer, please tell me about your picture."
Jennifer said, "I am drawing a picture of God."
"But, Jennifer," the teacher replied, "no one knows what God looks like."
Jennifer stood up, looked right at the teacher, and most assuredly said,
"In a few minutes, when I am done with my drawing,
everyone will know what God looks like."

Despite young Jennifer's assurance, it is impossible for us, mere mortals, to know what God looks like.

But perhaps we can open our ears and our hearts and begin to imagine what God might say to us. After all, if we are Earthly companions of the Divine, we might expect to hear from God now and then.

Let's pretend that one fine spring evening, we are walking our dog in the green, green grass of a lovely park among the stately trees and the wildly beautiful flowers. A cool breeze softens the heat of the day. And, there—walking the Divine dog, Fido—is God.

Awestruck and a bit intimidated, we nevertheless want to be polite and friendly. "Good evening, God," we might say. "Fido is looking very fine tonight, and You, God, You are looking very well."

"Good evening to you, My precious children. How are you?"

"Just fine, God, just fine. Thank You for asking. And, how are *You?*"

"Well, My children, let Me tell you. I am very proud of you. Much of the time, I rejoice in you. You are doing a great job as My companions on Earth.

"You discover, and invent, and make, and shape, and develop, and sustain, and partner with Me building a continually evolving and enlivened Earth. With the animation of your minds and spirits, your imagination, ingenuity, and the dedicated work of your hands and hearts, you enhance, enrich, enlighten, and ennoble the Earth.

"You can be—and very often are—kind, caring and compassionate, grace-full and elegant, just and good. When you touch hearts and hands with each other and when you embrace all that I have taught you, you move Earth toward its ultimate perfection."

What a compliment from God! "Thank You, God," we say. "Thank You very much. We are so glad that You are happy with us."

"Yet ..." says God.

What?

When God says "Yet," it is usually not very good news.

Our hearts seem to skip a beat and our stomachs begin to churn.

"Yes, God? What is it?"

"Come," says God. "Let's sit on that bench over there. We'll talk some more."

"My dear, dear ones," God continues, "it breaks My heart to say this, but sadly—oh so sadly—I may have to admit that the Angels who begged me not to create you might have been right. Far too often, I have been disappointed over your foolishness and folly. And I have wept bitter tears.

"Look. Look at the stunning beauty of this park—grass, trees, flowers, the placid lake, the chirping birds, the hopping bunnies, the squirrels with their fat little cheeks. And all the good folks walking their dogs, chatting with each other, laughing, and having a sweet evening. Does it remind you of anything?"

"Well ..." we say slowly, not quite understanding what God is asking. "Well ..."

"Oh, My precious children. How easy it is for you to forget. Not that I blame you, for you are just caught up in the realities of living on this Earth. But, if you dig deep, deep into your soul's memory, you will remember that this is what it was like when you were in the Garden. Beauty. Harmony. Tranquility. Companionship. Love. Paradise. Eden.

"That was our beginning together.

"I created you all to be one big human family—connected and unified in purpose; loving each other and Me.

"I made you, and I created the essence of your human nature. I know you. To help you live on Earth with each other, I gave you a set of simple rules for human behavior and told you the consequences of following or of violating that code.

"I gave you Eden on Earth—the place that was to be a perfect home for all of you.

"Yet, sadly—oh so sadly—you shattered Paradise. You separated from Me and disconnected from each other. You split into thousands of fiefdoms, spread out to myriad places on Earth. Your common speech became a babble of diverse language-sounds so you could not even communicate clearly with each other. And it was not long before your failings and faithlessness began to fill the Earth.

"Despite human sensibilities toward the good, the evil inclination often prevails. You can be petty and petulant, harsh and cruel. You lie, and cheat, and deceive, and steal, and murder. You demonize and marginalize 'The Other'—anyone who is different from you. You fight for wealth, and power, and prestige, and territory. You can be hate-mongers and war-mongers. You can wantonly devastate and blithely destroy.

"Your disconnection and separation from The Other—and from

Me—has brought you pain, anger, and hatred. You have played out your enmity with each other so often that your individual and collective blood cries out from My Earth on which you spilled it. Your guilt shouts out from the lands you have denuded, and the skies and waters you have polluted.

"Instead of always elevating the human spirit, you so often crush it.

"You fail to nurture and nourish your inherent greatness.

"Sometimes you try to rationalize and explain away your behavior. At other times, you are thrown to your knees by the consequences of your transgressions against the best that you know is within you."

Our heads bow and our eyes fill with tears.

What have we done? What have we done?

How have we made God so deeply disappointed in us?

Have we really ravaged and wrecked God's glorious world?

This is how God sees us?

This is how God feels about us?

"We're so sorry, God. We're so sorry. We didn't mean it to be this way. We didn't mean to offend You or make You sad.

"What can we do? What can we do to fix what we have broken, to make it all better? What can we do to make You happy with us again?"

God looks at us with such kindness and concern. For even in sadness and anger, God is always benevolent and loving. With Divine chastisement comes Divine comfort. God catches our tears and enfolds us in Divine Love.

So, God says, "My sweet and precious children, you are wise and you are strong. In your heart of hearts you know what is right. And you know that there are ways to fix what is wrong, ways to become the very best you can be, ways for you and Me to save our beautiful Earth before it is too late."

DEAR ONES

Dusk begins to fall as we sit on the bench with God, and the cool breeze begins to turn a bit chilly. Are we shivering because of the change in the weather, or because of what we are hearing from God?

We wait ... and wait.

And then, slowly, God begins to speak again.

"In days of old, and surely, these days, your theme song seems to be, 'My God's better than your God.'

"But that is absolutely impossible!

"There is only One God.

"Me.

"I am the Creator and Parent of each and every one of you.

> *I Am God. There is nothing else. I form light and create darkness. I make peace and create evil. I, the Source and Substance of All do this.* (Isa. 45:6–7)

"I am the Everything of the Everything, the wholeness, the totality, the Oneness of the universe—male and female, father and mother, light and dark and shadow, us and other, justice and compassion, pain and comfort, sense and nonsense, good and evil, anger and tranquility, indifference and passion, joy and sorrow, tragedy and triumph, right and wrong, yes and no, conflict and harmony, war and peace, vengeance and incredible love, life and death, and life eternal.

"There is nothing that is not Me.

"And I know you intimately and intensely.

> *Before I created you in the womb, I selected you;*
> *Before you were born, I consecrated you.* (Jer. 1:5)

"So, I tell you:

"Your two different genders are just a practicality so that you can reproduce and populate the Earth. Otherwise, men and women are equally human, equally My children.

"Your sexuality is your choice. I am All, and All is of Me. Every one of you is created in My Image. I do not care how you express your Beingness.

"Your so-called 'different' physical traits and characteristics are trivial. Your differences of skin, or eye, or hair color mean nothing. Your science has taught you: more than 99 percent of the makeup—what you call DNA—of all people of Earth is exactly the same.[1]

"Your physicality, your inherent capabilities, your perceived strengths or weaknesses, are insignificant. The place where you came into this Earth, where you were born—with your ethnicity, family, religion, culture, economic situation, and politics—and surely can influence your life, but makes little difference in who you are at your core.

"How do I know all this?

"When I created you, I made each one of you a perfect human being. I do not make mistakes.

"I gave you the whole Earth as your collective home.

"It is you who have imposed any perceived differences on each other. When you needlessly, and incorrectly, place separations between you, you set up false boundaries and bitter confrontations.

"Know this, My children. Know it well:

"I love you all—fully and equally.

"You are all My children.

"I do not play favorites.

"I love you all.

"In each era, I gave you a collection of myths, legends, fables, stories, codes, ways of living, and—most of all—ways to love.

"To the Hebrews, I gave the Bible.

"To the Christians, I gave the New Testament.

"To the Muslims, I gave the Koran.

"To the people of the East, I gave sacred ideas.

"To the indigenous peoples of all places, I gave tribal tales.

"All of these holy texts came through sages who were My messengers.

"Wisdom is wisdom. It does not belong to any one faith or religious community. It belongs to the universe—to all times and all places and all peoples.

"Yet ...," says God, "you all misunderstood. You all perverted My intent.

"Historically, and for many today, My religious guidebooks are seen not as cumulative but as superseding the previous.

"You all think that the Hebrew Bible is superior to the codes of the 'pagans' who came before the Jews.

"Christians think that the New Testament is 'replacement theology' of the Hebrew Bible.

"Muslims think that the Koran is superior to and supersedes both the Hebrew Bible and the New Testament.

"Your theory is that newer must be better, that newer revelation is better than older revelation, that I choose a new group to receive the newer, better teachings, and thus that new group must be superior to the older ones.

"Throughout your history, and now, for some who believe this way, it was/is not enough to claim theological supremacy over both the ideas and the people who proclaim them—but, because of your sincere belief that what you have is so much better than what has been, you want to force your beliefs on others.

"This has led to your theological, ideological, cultural, and political warfare—to crusades, nationalism, fundamentalism, radicalism, inquisitions, holy wars, pogroms, gas chambers, genocide, and worldwide terror—with the current threat of nuclear annihilation hovering.

"It has led to the disruption of the sacred relationship of human beings and Me as co-creative partners on this Earth. Our Earth cannot be healed, built up, and perfected while some are trying to tear it down through their own egoism and selfishness.

"Your sage so rightly said, 'When you make your particular religion your God, you lose the God of your religion.'[2]

"Your sense of supremacy and triumphalism is poisoning the world.

"The absolute, universal truth is: No group's book, no group's interpretation of Me, is superior to any other.

"Surely, there can be wide differences in beliefs and practices; in geographic, ethnic, and cultural backgrounds; and, some would even say, in characteristics that are passed through the generations.

"What you call *religion* came into being to be a vessel, a vehicle for people to join together to relate to Me—a power greater than you understood—and to attempt to find your place and purpose in the universe.

"Even though they may seem so different, each religion that you invented as your pathway to Me is nothing more than a reflection of the time, place, culture, politics, and social circumstances in which a particular religion was born and began to develop.

"In their purest form, your organized religions can be enlightening, embracing, sweet, uplifting, and inspiring.

"Yet, perversely, organized religion can be rigidly fundamental, confining, stifling, and punishing.

"Belief in Me—a relationship with Me—is a spiritual connection, a journey into My World of Spirit, the pathway to a personal, intimate loving relationship between you and Me.

"Every belief and faith community and the rites and rituals and ceremonies you form are right for you. Come with words; come with chant; come with dance; come with silence. You are all on the same journey—from Me to Me. Actually, there is great beauty in the different ways you walk the pathway, build the bridges, and make the journey. I appreciate them all.

"I do not care what you call Me. In a family, one child may call the male parent, Dad; another may say, Pop; still another, Father. One may say, Mother; another, Mommy; another, Mama. It does not matter, for each is referring to and addressing the same one parent.

"It is the same with Me. Call Me God; call Me Adonai; call Me Jesus; call Me Allah; call Me Vishnu or Shiva; call Me the Buddha; call Me by any of the hundreds and hundreds of names you have given Me.

"Call me what you will, but know that there is only One Me—the One God who is your One and Only Parent.

"You are all My children. I love you all.

"And I hope that you will love Me.

"Most of all, I hope that you will learn to love each other.

"There is much more that unites you as My children than divides you.

"Bigotry, racism, misogyny, nationalism, and xenophobia have gotten you nowhere. Hatred, violence, terror, genocide, and warfare have torn apart your Earth.

"The pathway to supporting the Earth is healing her wounds and affirming your places as My co-creative partners; to be in full consciousness of the Divinity of all.

"Your shared humanness means that you are all united in origin, purpose, and destiny. What happens to One happens to All.

"I am the One God.

"There is this One World in which we exist.

"You are One—children of Me—the One God.

"You—We—are One.

"All is One. One is All.

"Understand: Oneness—human unity—does not mean 'sameness.' Our world's richness comes from the dazzling tapestry of the ways that you live and become. There is so much to celebrate in your unique world-views and experiences.

"As I do, you, too, can see the worth and beauty in diversity, and at the same time celebrate the unity of humankind as children of the One God. You can cherish your magnificent uniqueness, and you can respect and honor the wondrous significance of all humankind.

"True Oneness is the shared journey of unity and harmony, peace and love.

"Love.

"Love is all there is.

"All is Love. Love is All.

"Do you understand, My precious children? Do you understand?"

With hearts overflowing and eyes filled with grateful tears, we nod, "Yes. We understand. And we will embrace Your sweet and loving teachings."

And right there—on that park bench—God leaned over and hugged us.

ACCEPT MY GIFTS

"There's one more thing that I want to tell you before I get back to overseeing the rest of the universe," says God.

"I Am asking you to accept My gift. Every day, every moment, I give you the gift of My continuing revelation. It is My way of speaking to new generations who have new languages, new learning, new wisdom, new experiences, new perspectives, new touchstones.

"My core teachings are universal and eternal. Most all the new teachings I give over to you are the result of your ever-unfolding world—with all its diversity, challenges, and possibilities. You know and understand much more of our vast universe. You have uncovered so many of the mysteries. You have tamed so many of the uncertainties. Much more than your ancient ancestors and even your grandparents and parents, you grasp My Divine Design for you.

"In your growth, you always need new pathways to journey, new vistas, new directions, a new summons. You need to enhance and enrich the past with the power of the present and the promise of the future.

"Please accept My continuing gifts, not with any haughtiness or self-proclaimed superiority, but with the humility and joy of knowing that each revelation is another portion that I give to all of you as your inheritance as My children on Earth.

"And please, whenever you might feel that tug of old thinking that you are better than any of your other brothers and sisters, please remember that you—all of you—are My precious children on Earth. I love all of you—each and every one of you. And I ask you to love each other."

ENTERING THE WORLD
OF SPIRIT

As sweet as it would be to sit on a park bench with God for a long time, God—and we—have to get back to living our lives. We can always be in touch, but we each have other things to do.

So, when we get back to the day-to-day of our lives and God goes off to keep running the universe, how do we stay in the incredible God-energy that we have just experienced on that park bench?

We enter into God's World of Spirit.

Many mystical traditions teach that we live on this Earth on four levels simultaneously—the physical, mental, emotional, and spiritual.

It takes certain skills, and luck, to interweave these four elements in order to navigate our lives successfully and enjoy the blessings that life can bring.

Yet what we encounter on this Earth is not all that is.

A dog hears the sound of a dog whistle inaudible to the human ear. Does that mean that the sound does not exist?

An AM radio can only receive AM signals. Does that mean that FM signals are not there?

A camera captures a picture that the lens is open enough to see. Does that mean that anything outside the lens's view is not there?

Are we to think that there is no more to this world than that which we can see, hear, and experience at this moment in time?

As the universe unfolds and divulges more and more of its secrets, we begin to see and embrace what has been there all the time but we had not yet developed the capacity to perceive.

Our task is to remember what we once knew and, in time, what we will know again.

> *Recently, a baby was born. When the parents brought her home from the hospital, the baby's four-year-old brother kept asking, "Can I be alone with my sister? When can the baby and I be alone?"*
>
> *The parents, not understanding why their son wanted to be alone with the newborn baby, and concerned about possible jealousy and sibling rivalry, kept putting off the request, saying, "It's good for all of us to be together." But the four-year-old was continually insistent, so the parents finally told him that he could go into the baby's room, and if he wanted privacy, he could close the door behind himself.*
>
> *Curious and a bit worried, the parents turned on the room's baby monitor so that they could hear what would happen. As soon as the door was shut, the four-year-old went up to the crib, looked right at his newborn sister and said, "Quick baby, tell me what I am supposed to remember. I'm forgetting already."*

Another story.

> *A young couple, parents of a three-year-old boy, told me that at his preschool their son had made very good friends with a little girl named Maddy. The parents were surprised because they thought that there were a number of other children whom their son might have chosen as best friend, but their Ollie was particularly drawn to Maddy and spent most of his time with her.*
>
> *On a hunch (or was it an intuition of knowing?) I asked Ollie, "Did you know Maddy from before?"*
>
> *"Sure," he replied matter-of-factly.*
>
> *"Where? When?"*
>
> *Ollie looked at me as if I were rather stupid asking such a simple question. He pointed his thumb upward and nonchalantly said, "When we were with God."[1]*

Tap into the memory of two-, three-, or four-year-olds, and they may be able to tell you about their preverbal infancy, their birth, perhaps about being in the womb, or they may even recount recollections of the World Beyond, because little children often remember what we have already forgotten—what it is to be on The Other Side in the World of Spirit, with God.

The English Romantic poet William Wordsworth poignantly reminds us: "Our birth is but a sleep and a forgetting ... and not in entire forgetfulness ... But trailing clouds of glory do we come from God who is our home ...."

Our souls are eternal. They hold cosmic knowledge of all time and space.

But the "rules" of being on Earth make it impossible for us to retain complete knowing. We forget; we cannot remember.

Still, there is always a faint light in the shadows. Every soul on Earth retains sparks of eternal knowledge, and every now and then we see a glimmer or a glimpse of what we once knew, an opening to All That Is.

Even as we revel in the experience of being embodied souls on Earth, our souls hold the memory of being on The Other Side, of holding universal knowledge, of being warm in the glorious light and the holy Presence of the Divine.

> I was once called to officiate at the funeral of a very fine elderly gentleman whom I did not know. When I was inquiring about his life so that I could pay proper tribute to him, his daughter said to me, "My father did not believe in God; there were no religious rituals or observances in our home, and he and Mother brought me up in the same way. I do not believe and I do not practice. So, I would like you to honor my father's beliefs and not mention the word 'God' at any time during the funeral service. And, my husband and I are bringing up our children in exactly the same way, so I ask you not to add to my children's grief over the death of their grandfather by confusing them with any God-talk."

This, of course, is no easy task for a rabbi with deep belief in the Divine, but I did not want to further add to the family's travails, so I agreed to be as sensitive as possible to the request.

I was waiting when the family arrived at the cemetery. The daughter and her husband got out of their car. Gently, they helped her mother, the new widow, into a wheelchair, and then their three children came out of the car—a fifteen-year-old girl, a ten-year-old boy, and a four- or five-year-old boy.

The little boy took about ten steps onto the cemetery grass, looked up at the sky, flung his arms wide open, and shouted "Hello, God!"

I thought his mother was going to fall into the open grave.

Our sacred task is to be consciously aware of what was, what is, and what will forever be.

Our daily mission and quest is to make the continuing journey from the rational, temporal Earth-world in which we live into the infinite World of Spirit in which our eternal souls forever exist.

True consciousness—real enlightenment—is the knowing that there is actually never any separation; there is only Oneness with God and the universe.

We know that we are a part of an ongoing continuum of time and space that has God at its very center. We know that we can be a conduit, a channel, from God to Earth and from Earth to God.

If we open our eyes wide and attune our ears sharply—if we watch and listen carefully to our daydreams and our night visions—we can be in the World of Spirit where the transcendent is manifest, where continuing revelation is always possible, and where consciousness evolves into the vastness of human potential.

In the World of Spirit is God.

In the World of Spirit is us.

BEING IN THE WORLD
OF SPIRIT

Since the Enlightenment, the world in which we live has put its highest value on matters of the mind—the highly intellectual, rational, logical, and, now, technological aspects of life. And surely, we have greatly benefitted from the discoveries and advances in thought, science, medicine, and technology that have flooded our world.

Yet even with the expertise of our own human role in these leaps forward, we know that there is nothing that is not of God, who is the Creator, Sustainer, Guide, and Redeemer of us and our world.

The Jesuit priest and spiritualist Pierre Teilhard de Chardin reminded us who we really are: "We are not human beings having a spiritual experience. We are spiritual beings having a human experience."

God placed us on this Earth with a Divine Design for our purpose and mission. We are to be co-creative partners in building up our world, and we are to follow God's code of moral behavior and ethical values that elevates the human spirit. With God, we are to fashion a world of goodness, righteousness, peace, and love.

God is at the very center of who we are, where we are, all that we are and what we do, and all that we will become.

With our teacher, Dr. Abraham Joshua Heschel *zt"l*, we know: "God is of no importance unless God is of supreme importance."

And we know: "We are God's stake in human history. We are the dawn and the dusk, the challenge and the test."

And surely, we know with happy certainty that:

"It takes three things to attain a sense of being:

God
A Soul
And a Moment

And the three are always here."

GOD WITHIN

It is not only the transcendent God of creation and history who speaks to us.

It is also the immanent God Within each and every one of us.

What makes the lump of chemicals that make up the human body into a breathing, living human being? We are taught that in the beginning God breathed the breath, the spirit of the Divine, into the first people—let's call them Adam and Eve. They came alive through God's breath, and their souls were made of "the light, the spark, of God" (Prov. 20:27).

The breath of God is within you.

God is within you.

There is no separation, no duality. God is the Fullness of All Being.

God breathes God's breath; you breathe your breath. But the breaths are not individual; they are not separate. You and God share one breath; you breathe the same breath together. God's Out-Breath is your In-Breath. Your Out-Breath is God's In-Breath. Can you imagine anything more intimate, anything more ardent?

We cannot take any breath for granted. For, not only is that breath the force and energy that keeps us in life, it is our recognition that God is within us. When we breathe with full cognizance and intention, we know with certainty that we are in connection with God and that we are part of the harmonic ebb and flow of the universe. Without our breath, the universe is incomplete. With our breath, all is in total alignment.

We are the loving partners with God in breathing the Beingness of all creation. We feel the immediate, close sweetness of entwinement with God.

And God Within is not only our life-animation; it is our conscience and our guide. Just as we all want to find, know, and be in deep relationship with the transcendent God, we want to touch God Within. We want to touch our Highest Selves, our God-Selves. We want to be Godlike—loving and compassionate, kind and caring. We want to be good and do good, to work for justice and righteousness. We want to be God's heart and hands here on Earth.

We want God to be at the very center of our being. We want to know God and be with God at the deepest level of our existence.

And God needs and wants all of us to be part of the Divine, to be wholly of God. God wants us to be in the "inside of the insides,"[1] to reside at the "Heart of all Being." You and I are Within God. We are at the very center of God's Being.

We seek to merge self with God's Self, being with God's Being. We want to come into alignment, attunement, *"at-One-ment"* with God. We want to be in the deepest spiritual intention and connection, the highest human consciousness. We want to be wholly present in God's design and flow, in God's energy field, God's light-sphere, God's wavelength. We want to be a conduit to God and a channel of God.

We each come into our God-Self when the channel between our small self and God-Full Source is completely open, so that God inundates our self with God. Our God-Self is our God-ness Within—the deepest, highest, and finest of our God-being.

> *Breath of all Breath,*
> *Life of all Life:*
> *I am of You.*
> *The one of the One.*
> *You are in me.*
> *The One of the one.*

From our deepest inner energy, we breathe the life force. We breathe God.

BUT I DON'T BELIEVE

It is only fair that we acknowledge and honor those of us who have difficulty with this God-talk, those who find it irrelevant, those who do not believe in God.

There are always challenges to God's place in this world.

Truth be told, there is not one of us who hasn't questioned, who, at one time or another, has not been a doubter, a skeptic. There are always rationalists and intellectuals who demand empirical and existential proof. There are always those who profess no faith. And there are always the faithful who sometimes wonder.

Age-old questions will not be easily settled, even in this new and ever-unfolding age. Few who do not believe or are doubtful skeptics will be moved to faith. Yet precisely because of the leaps of understanding that have been made in these years of enlightenment, many of the God mysteries of antiquity are continually and powerfully answered by the advances of modernity.

For some, the so-called existence of God is a simple childlike fantasy that has been made up by people attempting to give some explanation to the creation and ongoing process of the universe. The claims of experiencing or communicating with God are just concocted to make some sense of the often-chaotic world in which we live, and an attempt by those in temporal power to regulate and control human behavior. The universe as we know it was created by the "Big Bang theory,"[1] and is a random collection of elements that permit life on this planet. There is no scientific or empirical proof for the existence of God. No one has ever seen or touched God.

In this age of high science, medicine, and technology, when so much genius and power is in human hands, when machines (made, we sometimes tend to forget, by human minds and hands) seem to hold powers even greater than humankind, it is often easy to disavow God or to repudiate God, or to reject God, or to think that God has become irrelevant—that humankind is greater than God.

> Said the monk, "All these mountains,
> and rivers and the earth and stars
> —from where do they come?"
> Said the master, "From where does
> your question come?"

Dr. Robert Jastrow, the late physicist, astronomer, and head of NASA, America's space program, put it elegantly: "The scientist has lived by the power of reason. He has scaled the mountains of ignorance, and is about to conquer the highest peak. As he pulls himself over the final rock, he is greeted by a band of theologians who have been sitting there for centuries."

A story. Or is it?

> Scientists came to visit God. They said: "God, we are sorry to tell you this. We don't need You anymore. The only thing that You could do that we could not do is create ex nihilo, to create out of nothing. But now, we have found the way to create human beings all by ourselves. Sadly, You have become irrelevant to us. So, we have come to say good-bye to You."
> God replied, "Really? You can do that? Please show Me."
> So one scientist bent down and picked up a clump of rich soil from the ground, and began to shape it and forge it into a human being.
> God watched for a moment and then said, "No, no, no. Use your own dirt."

It is only God who gives us life.
And, it is only God who takes away our breath so that we die and

return to whence we came. Yes, human beings have the dubious power to kill in numerous ways. Genocide, and war, and hatred, and the lust for power and control, and the lack of regard for the sanctity of human life, and even medical error can bring death. Yet it is only God who holds the power to end human life in the pure ebb and flow of natural order.

An old story updated for contemporary times.[2]

> *A man was walking in a shopping mall in Los Angeles when he saw the Angel of Death standing in front of him. The Angel raised up its massive wings as if to embrace and take the man, so the man turned and ran for his life. He came home and told his children what had happened and then announced that he was immediately making an airplane reservation to fly to Chicago to avoid the Angel of Death.*
>
> *After he left for the airport, his children went to the mall to find the Angel of Death and inquire as to why their father was to die.*
>
> *When they found the Angel of Death they asked, "Why did you raise your wings to take our father? He is such a good man; he doesn't deserve to die now, especially here in this sterile, impersonal shopping mall."*
>
> *And the Angel of Death replied, "I did not raise my wings to take your father. It was just that I was so surprised to see him here. You see, I have an appointment with him tonight in Chicago."*

Science creates nothing anew. Science profoundly, yet merely, discovers what God already created during the first moments of Creation. Everything the world would ever have or need is already here, floating in the universe, waiting to be found. It is up to human beings to "stand on the shoulders" of those who came before us, rise up, and pluck out the already-here information. Discovery is the product of the human mind. And who gave human beings the mind to form thoughts and ideas, to be creative and inventive? God.

We see a universe that is perfectly formulated. Elephants give birth to elephants, oranges give birth to oranges, human beings give birth to human beings. The flap of a butterfly wing here affects the Earth across the globe. The forces of nature play out even when they cause consternation, harm, and tragedy to humans who either get in the way or who may be innocent bystanders.

There are always anomalies and defects that arise, for once the perfect plan manifested on Earth, it became subject to the vicissitudes of Earth life: the intersection of disparate elements; the capriciousness of human interaction; and the faithlessness, arrogance, and hubris that can ruin even the most sublime gift. Yet our continuing discovery and exploration of human DNA, and by extension, the DNA of the entire universe, is growing proof that a universe this perfect cannot possibly be the result of random chance. It is the carefully calculated plan of the Creator, God.

Just as there is a larger story, a plan and a purpose for the universe, there is a plan and a purpose for human beings. Science is neutral; it is neither good nor bad. Science has no value-sourced mandate, no moral code or judgment. But God placed human beings on this Earth to build and sustain a moral, ethical universe, centered in God-given standards for human behavior.

God, who created us, completely understands the human condition, and gave us our Creator's grandest hopes and expectations for humankind. This ethical mandate teaches us the underlying principle of our existence: how to love God, how to love each other, how to love ourSelves. This is the intention and the purpose—and the *glory* of our creation.

> *To follow the ways of God*
> *To do the right and the just.* (Gen. 18:19)

Yes. There is evil and suffering in our world. God never promised anyone a life without anguish or pain. Life happens. Sometimes it is exhilarating and joyous; sometimes it is sad and sorrow-filled. Evil and suffering are a part of life, because evil and suffering are a part of God, and thus part of humankind. No one is immune or exempt. The Bible's suffering servant Job asked, "Shall we receive good from God's hand, but not evil?" (Job 2:10).

> *The son of an ancient sage became very ill and fell into a deep coma. His holy father sat by his bedside praying for him with deep devotion.*
>
> *According to God's plan, the young man awoke and began to recover.*
>
> *His father said to him, "Tell me, my son: When you were hovering between worlds — when your precious soul was lingering between This World and The World to Come —what did you see?"*
>
> *The son said, "I saw a world turned upside down. It was topsy-turvy."*
>
> *His wise old father said to him, "My son, you have seen* this world *as it really is."* (BT Pesachim, 50a)

Most of the evil in the world—the events that affect us so adversely—is caused by human beings. Human beings persecute, torture, and kill. Human beings commit genocide and make war. Human beings harm each other and cause havoc with each other's lives.

The solution to human upon human evil is: Stop! Love instead of hate. Care instead of disdain. Be kind instead of nasty. Have compassion. Have grace. Make peace, not war.

Speak up. "Silence encourages the tormentor, never the tormented."[3]

And, please. Always remember: "All that is necessary for the triumph of evil is when good men do nothing."[4]

Become a Messenger of Peace. Become a Warrior for Good.

Another kind of what we call evil is what the insurance companies call "acts of God"—earthquakes, floods, fires, tornadoes, hurricanes. These happenings are simply natural acts of God's universe. There is nothing inherently evil about them. They just are. They become evil to us when human beings get in the way—when homes, cities, and lives are destroyed.

The solution to nature's acts of so-called evil is two-fold. First, we can use human discernment to prevail before any destruction takes place. Do not build homes in the path of what we know are California wildfires. Do not build cities on earthquake fault lines. Do not plant corn fields in flood plains. Do not live in lowlands where rivers always overflow or storms bring high waves. It may be beautiful or productive to live in certain locales, but it may not be wise.

If that seems too impractical or far too late to change long-established reality, then use human ingenuity to tame the monsters. Develop fireproof materials to construct housing. Put skyscrapers on ball bearings so they will sway in the earthquake instead of falling. Build higher and higher dams, dykes, and seawalls to contain the flood waters and the crashing waves. Humankind has already taken major steps in this direction, and continued creativity and innovation will bring us closer and closer to diminishing the negative effects of random acts of nature.

Just as so many are working to overcome the natural acts of the universe, medical and technological science is working daily to discover the remedies and the cures for disease. The expected human life span has grown tremendously over the past century due to incredible advances in diagnosis and treatment. Other scientists have found ways to alleviate pain and suffering; further preserve human dignity; and give comfort to the ill, those who care for them, and those who care about them.

Into most every life come pain and suffering. Disease and illness are at one time or another part of almost every life. Death is inevitable. The truth of our existence is that, even though we are saddened, we have more or less made peace with the natural order of life and death when a person dies at age one hundred. We are outraged and crestfallen when a young person dies or suffers debilitating accident or illness. We rail against what seems to us to be the topsy-turvy, upside-down randomness of the universe.

We do not know God's Design for our world. We do not know how our temporal suffering fits into the Divine plan and how our personal pain may be contributing to the ultimate perfection of the world.

And so, we look to an ancient story in the book of Genesis for wisdom:

> *In the biblical story, Joseph's brothers caused him harm. In the pit where they threw him and in the Egyptian prison where he was confined, Joseph was not a happy man.*
>
> *Through a series of unlikely events, he rose to great position and power in Egypt. When his brothers finally came to meet him again, they were afraid that he would take revenge on them for their transgressions against him.*
>
> *But Joseph said, "You meant it for evil against me. But God meant it for good."* (Gen. 50:20)

And it was good indeed, for because of the position Joseph ultimately attained in Egypt, he was able to save an entire country from starvation and his whole family from certain death.

Because we are human, because we have human feelings, we deeply experience the pain of separation, loss, and anguish. Our ultimate response determines their power over us. How we react—how we are affected physically, emotionally, and spiritually is up to us. Will we be victims? Or triumphant survivors? It all depends on what our heads, hearts, and spirits choose.

Surely, even in our darkest moments, we cannot reject or even ignore God. For real trauma, real anguish and angst, real existential loneliness come when we disconnect and separate from God. But as long as we stay connected to God, as long as we remain in alignment with God, as long as we stay at-One with God, we remain in accord with our soul's Earth-mission in this human sojourn, and in harmony with the universe. Together, we and God can face anything and prevail.

As a good parent, God feels our pain and weeps with us. So, we can turn to God for comfort and strength. The psalmist of old gives us direction: "From out of the depths, I called out to God. From out of the great expanse of God's goodness, God answered me"—and lifted me up. "God heals the shattered heart and binds up the wounds" (Ps. 118:5, 147:3).

Yes. There are other organizing systems for human life and interaction. Many are classified as "isms." Some *isms* have been very valuable to the process and the progress of the world. Others, while attracting passionate adherents, have narrowed the worldview. And certain *isms* have brought great destructive harm: anarchism, authoritarianism, Marxism, fascism, Nazism, racism, Stalinism, communism, utilitarianism, hedonism, nihilism, materialism, secularism.

Have any of these *isms* brought the world any closer to harmony, peace, and love? Has any one of these ultimately brought us closer to understanding the world, giving deeper connection to something beyond or greater than self, bringing happiness and soul-satisfaction?

The *isms* lack any authority other than the power that is obtained or granted to their articulators and main purveyors.

While surely, throughout history, there have been many grievous perversions and violations of God's word and will, the test of time proves that faith-based systems, especially those with ethical value systems at their core, still have the best chance to help forge a just and peaceful world and bring personal contentment.

One of the *isms* that seems to command the most attention in today's world is Zionism, the religious-political movement that led to the establishment and continues to support the modern State of Israel.

There is much history, both ancient and modern, that informs the contemporary conflict and the lack of a solid and secure peace for Israel and her neighbors. Ironies abound in the opposing narratives, passions run wild, hearts are hardened, and opportunities to make peace have slipped away time and time again.

While I—as a Jew, a rabbi, and a passionate Zionist—would love to argue "our side," it is not for us to litigate the issues here, neither within each group nor between the groups.

Yet, from our perspective, the issue of Israel goes far beyond the existence of the modern State. We echo the words of Rabbi Lord Jonathan Sacks *zt"l* to Great Britain's House of Lords: "'We don't hate Jews,' they said in the Middle Ages, 'just their religion.' 'We don't hate Jews,' they said in the nineteenth century, 'just their race.' 'We don't hate Jews,' they say now, 'just their nation state.'"

The core of any discussion about the modern State of Israel begins in the two-millennia-old moral disease of anti-Semitism.

Still, here, it is only ours to set the narratives and conflict into a different direction.

A solution can only begin to emerge when, first, all parties (and particularly the extremists on all sides) stop advocating the destruction of lands and the annihilation of peoples; and when all parties agree to recognize each other and each other's right to exist in secure, defensible borders. This can happen only when there is honorable self-determination and abiding respect for human rights for all—including religious, ethnic, and civic minorities; women; and the most vulnerable members of these societies.

The thirteenth-century, mystic poet Rumi, whose teachings are being rediscovered and celebrated today, put it most powerfully: "Out beyond the ideas of wrongdoing and rightdoing, there is a field. I will meet you there."

This is true not only for Israel and her neighbors, but for all nations of the world. The political dynamic is the same everywhere where countries are in conflict with each other.

Yet if neither a political nor practical resolution can be achieved, then the only hope that peace will come to Israel and her neighbors is a Divine intervention—a miracle from God.

A miracle is a natural event that takes place at exactly the right place and at exactly the right time.

Who best knows the right time?

God.

And God knows that we need a miracle.

As the eighteenth-century, British poet and politician Lord Byron said when asked during a theology examination at Cambridge to explain the miracle of conversion of water into wine, "The water met its Master and blushed."

All of us—every person of peace and good will in this world—need to call out to God: Split the seas of enmity and hatred. Bring the dry land of safety and security. Let freedom ring out and stability be established. Deliver us into the Promised Land of healing, harmony, and peace.

And God will say to us,

> *"I hear your prayer and I say to you:*
> *I Am the Parent of you all. Isaac and Ishmael are*
> *both my sons. Jacob and Esau are both my sons.*
> *You—all of you who live in the holy lands—are the*
> *descendants of both sides of one family. You are brothers*
> *and sisters; you are cousins. Stop your sibling rivalries.*
> *Stop your fights over who is closer to Me, who is My*
> *favorite, who gets My rightful inheritance.*
> *You are all my children. I love you all.*
> *Respect each other. Care about each other. Love each other.*
> *I may seem to be the Miracle-Maker.*
> *But the real miracle is in you.*
> *Make peace, not war.*
> *Meet Me in My Holy City of Jerusalem and touch hands*
> *in love and peace.*
> *Shalom. Salaam. Pax. Peace."*

For all of us, our understanding of God and the universe is still limited to what we know and perceive at this moment.

God's ultimate ways remain a mystery wrapped in an enigma.

Not knowing the fullness of God makes us human. It does not mean that God does not exist. It does not mean that we can reject or ignore God. It does not mean that we should not continue to engage and sometimes wrestle with God. It does not mean that we should not love God.

We may wish for God to use Divine power to wave a "magic wand" to right the wrongs, to protect us from harm and sorrow, to rid us of our troubles; rather, we know that God *empowers us* to bring righteousness, goodness, and love into our world.

For, in Dr. Heschel's words, we know, if only we would listen and heed, that: "The word of God never comes to an end. No word is God's last word."

As our human consciousness grows, as we discern and unfold more and more of God's intent, we are able to enlarge the storehouse of human understanding, knowledge, and feeling. So many of the secrets of the universe have already been uncovered. More revelation is sure to come. Every day, every moment, God gives over more and more mysteries of the universe and reveals deeper truths.

What our souls once knew, we will know again on This Side or on The Other Side. For, we are always God's precious children; we are ever in God's safekeeping.

We recall the words of United Nations Secretary General and 1961 Nobel Peace Prize Laureate Dag Hammarskjold: "On the day I first really believed in God, for the first time, life made sense to me and the world had meaning"—and the wisdom in Psalms 27:14, "Look to God. Be strong and of good courage. Yes! Look to God!"

You are with God.
God is with you.
You are within God.
God is within you.
Heaven and Earth touch.
It is Eden once again.

From God.
To God.
The Gates are always open.
The Bush always burns.
Without Beginning.
Without End.

Come.
EveryThing,
EveryWhere,
EveryOne
awaits.

WHAT DO YOU
REALLY WANT?

Most human beings want the same thing. Food. Shelter. Clothing. Good health. A sense of purpose. Education. Productive work. Prosperity. Friendship. Love. Happiness. For some, children and grandchildren. Inner peace. A meaningful existence. A life of decency and dignity. A worthy legacy.

If we want all these things for ourselves, then how much more do we want them for our children and our children's children and generations yet unborn.

And most of us think that this is what God wants for us too.

We are saddened when we see people who think that accumulation of wealth and communal standing, and establishing influence and power, will bring satisfaction through prominence and prestige—even if it takes cutthroat business practices, ruthless competition, and unfettered greed.

And in so many ways we see the world diminished when we witness that the greatest motivation of big business and multinational corporations (with some notable and praiseworthy exceptions) is making huge profits, accumulating wealth, and gaining territorial and political power and prestige.

Add to this the shadow-secrets that exist when there are so many actions hidden from public view by the wealthiest and most powerful people in the world who use their fortunes to manipulate and attempt to control the world for their own purposes.

There is nothing wrong with striving for monetary gain. It is in many ways a measure of success. It provides for the necessities and perhaps some of the luxuries of life. And happily, good and well-meaning people often use their wealth to promote and support worthy causes.

Yet, all too often, self-serving people and entities darken the world's pursuit of Oneness and fragment the journey toward love.

My reality: Every time I have visited a seriously ill person and every time I have prayed with a dying person, no one has ever said to me, "I wish I had spent more time on my business. I wish that I had bought a fancier house, more cars, better golf clubs. I wish that I had gotten more degrees, more titles, more awards."

No. Sick and dying people have said to me, "I wish I had spent more time with my wife/husband/partner. I wish I had spent more time with my children—more baseball games, dance recitals, camping trips, campus visits—more playing with the grandchildren. I wish I had spent more time at my synagogue, church, mosque, temple. I wish I had spent more time volunteering in my community, helping where I could. I wish that my family will remember me for my presence, not for my absence, and my friends will remember me for how much I cared about their lives. I wish that I will be remembered not for getting but for giving. I wish that my children will count their inheritance not in money, but in how much I loved them."

Why should every human being not want the same thing? Why should self-interest and self-aggrandizement override the personal need for a life of satisfaction and honor and for the collective need for a world of love and loving kindness?

How do we get what we really want—what we and our world need the most?

How do we live worthy and worthwhile lives and attain what is really important to us and right for the entire world?

We open our eyes and see.

There are still far too many who are left on the outside looking in.

Ambition, hard work, and devotion to achieving a life well-lived all too often are thwarted by the ills of society—racism, discrimination, the cycle of poverty, the drug culture, and the violence that erupts when dreams are shattered and hopes are crushed.

Once, a while ago, President Lyndon B. Johnson (from 1963–1969) declared a "War on Poverty." Tragically, in all too many places, poverty won. We found that there was no magic formula to cure the ailments that beset us.

It is now up to us to reverse the failure. Those who "have" can— and must—find the prescription to boost up those who "have not." There does not have to be a socialist- or communist-driven imperative for total equality. But there can be a formula that enables us to move toward a coequal and just existence.

An economically segregated society is no longer acceptable. And it is no longer tolerable that so many people do not have what they need and want.

From the depths of our knowing, the Voice of God speaks to us: "My precious children. I have given you all the resources you need to provide for and take care of yourselves. You have the ability to have all you want—not just for the few, but for all—if only you will truly understand that I made all of you, and that I want the best for each of you, and that you can use the talents I have given you to care for and about each other.

"If you have been blessed with good fortune, please share your bounty.

"If you have been blessed with prosperity, please share your resources.

"If you have been blessed with contentment, please share your joy.

"And to My sweetest children—if you do not have what you want, if you often face disappointment, if you feel left out or beaten up by life—please hold My hand.

"If your spirits have been broken by the vicissitudes of life, together we can revive them.

"If your souls have been soiled by the grime and pollution of life, together we can purify them.

"If your hearts have been hardened by the disillusionments and sorrows of life, together we can soften and heal them.

"How?

"Trust in yourSelves. Trust in each other. Trust in Me.

"Be strong and of good courage.

"Together, we can overcome."

God is not like Santa Claus, whom we can ask for worldly possessions, good grades on a test, or victory for our favorite sports team. God is our guide and our protector. God provides strength, courage, direction, and vision for our journey, and sets us on the pathway to self-determination and accomplishment.

And God reminds us that, ultimately, success is not measured by what we have, but by who we are—solid in our sense of Self and filled with soul-satisfaction.

What a world it would be if every person could know with absolute certainty that there is no need for competition or dominance or a lust for power, but that there is more than enough in this world for every human being to have everything we each need and desire, and to live in love and peace.

WHAT DOES GOD WANT?

To make our lives into what we can really be, can we perceive what God wants for us and for our world?

An old adage teaches:

"God desires the heart."

"God wants a pure heart" (BT San. 106b, Ps. 24:4).

How do we know how to fully and gladly give God our hearts? How do we know how to fashion a pure heart?

We can open our minds and our souls to the teachings that God has given us throughout the ages and to the sweet talks we have with God on the Garden's bench.

With certainty, we can say what God *does not want*. God does not want God's children fighting with each other over petty and insignificant matters. God does not want God's children fighting over religion. And—for God's sake—God does not want God's children fighting and killing each other over God, or over what one or another perceives is God's favoritism or imprimatur.

God wants each human being to become the best he/she can be.

God wants each human being to live free from need and fear, with all-encompassing human rights and dignity.

God wants the fulfillment of the original Divine dream that Earth be overflowing with goodness and love, and that all God's children dwell in peace and harmony.

And from all of our wisdom literature and from our own inherent knowing, we can discern that:

God does not want tyranny. God wants freedom.

God does not want debasement. God wants dignity.

God does not want falsehood. God wants truth.

God does not want perverted "truth." God wants ultimate and eternal truth.

God does not want division. God wants unity.

God does not want separation. God wants connection.

God does not want discord. God wants harmony.

God does not want isolation. God wants community.

God does not want strife. God wants tranquility.

God does not want depravity. God wants decency.

God does not want apathy. God wants compassion.

God does not want brokenness. God wants wholeness.

God does not want despair. God wants hope.

God does not want unconsciousness. God wants awareness.

God does not want rejection. God wants embrace.

God does not want discrimination. God wants acceptance.

God does not want danger. God wants safety.

God does not want fear. God wants security.

God does not want dark, hidden secrets. God wants the bright lights of revelation.

God does not want wrong. God wants right.

God does not want evil. God wants good.

God does not want war. God wants peace.

God does not want hate. God wants love.

When we choose to live the values and virtues that God wants, our lives reflect the Divine Desire. Then we may live long—and well—and prosper.

A caution: We have to be very careful not to assume that what we claim God wants is but simply our own desires. We cannot be limited to the view of our own experiences, our temporal boundaries of finite existence, our Earthly cravings and selfishness, and especially our own interpretations of God's will.

President Abraham Lincoln put it this way, "I humbly pray that I am on God's side."

"Thy will be done." (Matt. 6:10)

God has given us the privilege and the power to make God's will into reality. And so: God asks us to heal brokenness and to restore the Earth to its original purpose—to be the Earthly reflection of the perfection of Paradise.

We can *do* good.

We can *be* good.

And we will be fulfilling God's will here on Earth.

We will be aligned with the Divine Design.

We will be giving God what God wants.

BUT WE ARE AFRAID

So why don't we *go for it*? Why don't we reach out for what we really want? Why don't we strive to get what God really wants for us? Why don't we take the risks and confront the challenges?

We are afraid.

Hard and harsh truth be told: We are afraid of anyone or anything that is different from us or foreign to us, incompatible with us, contrary to us. We fear "The Other"—an idea, a value, a person, a community, a nation—that is unlike our own. We fear challenge and change that threatens our beings and our existence.

It used to be that some of us could count on the institutions and systems that held our little part of the world steady and firm. We had faith in our schools, our banks, our doctors and hospitals, our government, our religious communities.

Now, much of what sustained us seems to be crumbling right before our eyes. Nothing is the same. We worry about our children's educations; our finances, pensions, and retirement; our health care; our fractured and broken government leaders and courts; our countries split into seemingly irreconcilable political factions. Even our churches, synagogues, mosques, and temples that once held the center and created a sense of community and social responsibility now seem to be losing focus and are becoming irrelevant to many.

Change is inevitable, and we are the witnesses and participants in a massive shift that portends the new, perhaps even axial, age that is coming. For some, this is extremely exciting as we plunge forward into new vistas and unimagined opportunities.

But many fear the unknown. This kind of world-shattering change challenges longstanding, comfortable, steadfast beliefs and behaviors. Our safer, surer world is falling apart. And we are afraid.

We are afraid because we have no idea what is coming next. We fear the uncertain, the unforeseeable, the unpredictable. We are afraid of the dark in which we sit before the new dawn.

That is why so many cling to what is already known, what is secure, what seems safe. The certainty and the comfort of the past shields against the bewildering and unsure possibilities of the future. Some people hang on as tightly as possible to what was, so they need not face what might be.

This rigid grip can lead to the kind of narrow thinking and stubborn inertia that keeps the world from moving forward. Most often they are political, and/or religious, and/or social conservatives, that is, Conservative *with a capital C*. They posit that their conservatism is the way to hold on to the known, comfortable past and to honor individuality and personal autonomy. Their views are countered by progressives, that is, Progressives *with a capital P*, who advocate robust diversity, shared social responsibility, and the celebration of the common good as hallmarks of the unfolding of the new world.

Sadly, it is not enough for fundamentalists or extremists—of every place on the ideological spectrum—to do so for themselves alone. They think it is their duty to convince all the rest of humanity to embrace their positions. They play on our fears. They insist that they, and only they, know the real Truth—that is, Truth *with a capital T*. So in essence they say: We are right about this. Our stance is the best. We are certain that it is best for you and for our world too. If you do not believe us, if you do not accept our worldview, then we will try to reason with you. If that does not bring you to our side, we will try to radicalize you. If that does not work, we will terrorize you. If that does not work, then with harsh words and terrifying deeds, we will strike out against you and kill you.

And so, we are afraid of the bullet in the noonday sun. We are afraid of the bombings of our buildings and subways; the mass shootings in our theaters, nightclubs, and places of worship; the vehicle attacks on our streets. We are outraged that our children's playgrounds have become killing fields. We are furious about the bomb threats against our preschools. We are insulted by the physical pat-down at airport security lines. We are brokenhearted by our loss of innocence. And we are afraid to stand up to radical fundamentalists, terrorists, or killers in our communities—lest we be declared their sworn enemies and become their new favorite targets.

Let's tell it like it is. Any group or person who tries to impose beliefs or behavior on others must be stopped from discrimination and intimidation. Everyone has a right to personal or communal belief and passion. No one has a right to force that belief or passion on anyone else.

Fundamentalism is poisoning our world. So mainstream, moderate Jews must stand up to the rigid ultra-Orthodox; mainstream, moderate Protestants must stand up to evangelicals; mainstream, moderate Catholics must stand up to arch-conservatives; mainstream, moderate Muslims must stand up to radicals. And mainstream moderates of every place on the gender, racial, and political spectrums must stand up to misogynists, white supremacists, neo-Nazis, neo-fascists, and anti-Semites. We can no longer let the "big, bad bullies" of this world terrorize us or control our lives. We can no longer be afraid.

There is only one antidote to fear: Love.

It will take love to overcome the fundamental hatreds and self-righteous sense of superiority that reside in some hearts. Love wipes away the fear and brings the light of understanding, tolerance, acceptance, and embrace.

We can send our love energy out into the world so that it can enter still-misguided hearts. We can make a world not of terror and fear, but of serenity and hope, love and peace.

The whole world is a narrow bridge.
The main thing is to not make yourself afraid.[1]

ALL IS LOVE—LOVE IS ALL

The Bible tells us that the Seraphim, the Great Angels in the Heavens, stand on both sides of the Throne of God and shout across to each other, *"Kadosh, Kadosh, Kadosh. Sanctus, Sanctus, Sanctus. Holy, Holy, Holy"* (Isa. 6:3). They are acknowledging and celebrating the uniqueness and the greatness of God.

That chanting creates the Love Vibration, which becomes the basic element of all Creation, sends the love of God directly to Earth, and infuses the entire world with Divine Love. That is why Rumi teaches that "Love has seven hundred wings, and each one extends from the Highest Heavens to the lowest place on Earth."

From the beginning of time, writers, poets, artists, dancers, composers, musicians, singers—and every human being who has felt a heart-flutter of connection—have tried to depict the idea, the meaning, the reality, of love. There are so many kinds of love—parent and child, sibling, grandparent, family, extended family, sexual partner, spouse, life partner, friend, animal, pet, nature, community, culture, country, God. Each love is different; all love is similar and familiar.

Despite our best efforts, words, songs, and pictures cannot possibly capture the feelings of one human heart and soul toward another. So we look for a way to describe the feeling, the sensation, the emotion, the process, the reason, and the wisdom of love in the best ways we can for ourselves in our time, our place, our language.

Since God, who created Everything, created love—and since the Love Vibration on our Earth comes directly from God's Heavenly Throne, we look to God to tell us about love.

"Love your enemy."

"Love the stranger."

"Love one another."

"Love your neighbor/companion as you love yourself."[1]

Or better, "Love your neighbor. He/she is just like you."

Defining love, in its many configurations, comes to this: "The ability to cherish others, to make their lives as dear to us as our own, to share their hopes, to feel their hurts, to know their hearts."[2]

One friend said to another, "Do you love me?"

"Of course, I love you."

"How am I feeling?"

"How do I know how you feel?"

"How can you say that you love me if you do not know how I feel?"[3]

*

A long time ago—or maybe it was yesterday—a woman's child was very ill. She was told that the only hope for the child was a blessing from a great sage who lived a long distance away. She hired a wagon with its horse and driver, and rode to the sage's home with her sick baby in her arms.

She said to the sage, "Please, please. My child is so very ill. I am told that you are the only one who can bring the blessing of healing. Please, master, please. Heal her."

The sage closed his eyes and swayed in prayer for a very long time. Then he turned to the woman and said sadly, "I am so sorry. There is nothing I can do for your child. There is no blessing I can give. The Gates of Heaven are shut tight."

Distraught, the woman grabbed her child, ran out of the sage's house, got back on the wagon, and instructed the driver to return to her home so that she and her dying child could be with the rest of the family.

It was not long before the woman heard hoofbeats coming

behind the wagon. She looked and there was the sage on his horse. She instructed the driver to stop the wagon, and waited for the sage to catch up with them.

"Have the Gates of Heaven opened?" she asked excitedly. "Has the decree changed? Will my child live?"

"I am so very sorry," replied the sage. "Nothing has changed. The Gates are still closed."

"Then why have you come here? If there is nothing you can do for me and my child, why have you come after us?"

The sage replied, "You left so quickly that I did not have time to cry with you." And the sage held the child in his arms and sat on the side of the road with the woman.

And, together, they wept all night.[4]

Love.

Love is complete, unequivocal, nonjudgmental, unconditional, unrestricted, unrestrained. Our love—given freely and fully—delights the heart, awakens the spirit, and transforms the soul.

Love transcends all limitations of time and place.

When there is doubt, our love brings trust.

When there is despair, our love brings hope.

When there is hurt, our love brings healing.

When there is grief, our love brings comfort.

When there is fear, our love brings confidence.

When there is anger, our love brings reconciliation.

When there is shame, our love brings reassurance.

When there is transgression, our love brings forgiveness.

When there is attraction, our love brings passion.

When there is satisfaction, our love brings contentment.

When there is achievement, our love brings celebration.

When there is triumph, our love brings jubilation.

When there is bounty, our love brings appreciation.

When there is happiness, our love brings joy.

What the world needs now is love.

The world is hungry—*desperate*—for the love that will speak to our battered hearts, heal our painful wounds, bring light to the dark places, and set us on the course toward goodness and light.

We can be enveloped in the Love Vibration.

We can be Love.

When we love each other, we bring love to the world.

When we love each other, we connect Heaven and Earth.

We can be inspired by the grave marker at the final Earth resting place of our teacher Reb Zalman *zt"l* that reads, "He loved us to God."

RADICAL LOVING

The Psalmist of old taught us how to love: "I place God before me always" (Ps. 16:8).

What does it mean to place God before me?

The slang of the day might say, "Put God in your face."

How do we do that?

Our physical density sometimes blocks our flow, so we often miss what our spiritual beings inherently know:

> Wherever we look, there is God.
> All we have to do is be aware, be conscious.
> God is Everything—Everywhere.

Turn here, there is God. Turn there, there is God.

Turn right, left, up, down, around—there is God.

Instead of seeing what seems to be right in our view—a tree, a car, a person—we can see God. When we see the face of another—animate or inanimate—we can see God.

Seeing your face is like seeing the Face of God. (Gen. 33:10)

We can see the Face of God in our most intimate partner, our precious children, our oldest and best friend, or in the person we just met. We can see the Face of God in the faces of our dearly-missed beloveds who have gone on to the Great Beyond; in the faces of our descendants yet unborn, who are our progeny; and in the face of every stranger on the street and every human being on this planet.

At times of greatest joy, we see God. In the face of our lover, in the accomplishment of our son, under the bridal veil of our daughter—we see God. At such moments, even before we see the glory of our own gladness and gratification, we see God.

At times of great challenge and sorrow—illness, perceived personal or professional failure, estrangement, divorce, death—if we put God between us and the obstacle, we see God. We all know people who have faced their illness and their death with calm and equanimity. We have heard of martyrs of every faith who have faced their fate with surrender and peace. We are aware of the holy ones who walked into the gas chambers and, even then, saw the face of God and sang of their belief in the coming of the Messiah. Instead of seeing impending doom, true believers see God.

Every day, in every life-circumstance, in every moment, we can see God.

In the face of another, we *can* see the Face of God.

Instead of fuming at the bank teller who seems to be taking forever to make the transaction, we can see God.

Instead of becoming utterly frustrated with the teenage clerk in the convenience store who cannot make change for a dollar without a computer, we can see God.

Instead of banging on the steering wheel in anger at the horrible driver who cuts across lanes in traffic, we can see God.

But what about the terrorist, the lone gunman, or the person shunned by society because of disability, severe mental illness, or stark differences of appearance or behavior? What about the one rejected by society because of race, religion, creed, or sexual identity? What about those who are unwelcome, isolated, alone, lonely, poor, hungry, homeless, without hope—and the ones who have given up?

What would it be if we could look into all those faces and see the Face of God—if we could look into all those faces and treat each person as the true child of God that he/she is?

When we see the Face of God, how can we react in any way except to be wrapped in love?

What would it be if, openly and freely, we gave each person intense, passionate, radical love?

Then we would know that every person is just like us, a child of God.

And instead of fear, frustration, disdain, or anger, we would offer love—God's love and ours.

We can see God in every human being. And to every one of them we can reflect the Face of God, and every one of them can reflect the Face of God to us.

How? How can we see the Face of God in the teller, the clerk, the driver, the terrorist, the warrior, the tyrant?

It seems much easier to feel disdain, anger, hatred—and, yes, *fear*. But we know: When we hate, when we fear, it goes out to the other, and then it comes right back at us. Instead of creating a circle of gentle love, we create a vicious circle of rancor. We create a continuing atmosphere of loathing and rejection. We ignore God's Love. We reject God.

But our task is to bring God's Love and Light into the world, to *be* God's Love and Light in the world. So we remember our request in one of our prayers. We ask God for grace, love, and compassion:

GRACE is unconditional, providential love. We get it just because we are God's children and God gives all of us unconditional love. We do not have to earn it, nor do we have to do anything special to receive it. Grace is *gratis;* grace is free. We get it just because God is God, and we are God's creation. As God gives Grace to us, we can give Grace to our fellow human beings.

LOVE is Covenantal Love. When we are born on Earth our souls have accepted a contract to be here and a mission to accomplish. This means we have entered into an agreement with God to be God's partners in the ongoing, daily recreating of our Earth. Some faith communities have ceremonies to proclaim or receive the Covenant. However, whether or not there is a formal ceremony, the Covenant is automatically in place. Because of this Covenant, we receive God's

Covenantal Love—the continual affirmation of the pledge and the promise between God and each one of us to move the Earth toward goodness and right. As God gives Love to us, we can give Love to our fellow human beings.

COMPASSION means to walk step by step with those who are suffering, those who need a caring companion at one or more points on life's journey.

First, we ask God for compassion, for we always need the helping hand of God to make our way through the maze of life.

Then we offer our compassion to God. It is not easy being God, so God appreciates our heartfulness.

When we have learned to receive and give with God, then we can offer our Compassion to our fellow human beings—any and every person who needs or desires it. We can become God's hands on Earth.

And finally, we can give our compassion to ourSelves, for who needs our compassion more than we do?

God's Face in our faces? Love given and received that can change the world? A naïve fantasy? Impossible?

Back in 1987 hundreds of thousands of idealistic people joined together, held hands across the world, and sang and prayed for love and peace. We called it the Harmonic Convergence. It was an attempt to change the world. And the world laughed.

What happened?

Over the next few years, the Berlin Wall came down and communism ended in the Soviet Union. Democracy, in one form or another, came to the Soviet satellite countries. Blacks and whites started riding the bus together in South Africa. Catholics and Protestants stopped shooting at each other in Northern Ireland. And, once in a while, Israelis and Arabs sit across from each other to talk about the possibility of peace.

Did a few people holding hands and singing songs make all these massive changes happen? Of course not. But we did send the Love

Vibration, the energy of loving change, out into the world, where it circled the globe and then it spiraled back into the heart of each and every person. We helped raised consciousness. We affirmed Oneness consciousness. And that changed the world.

What the world needs now is *Love Beyond Love—Radical Loving*. Radical Loving is:

- the absolute recognition and celebration that God loves us with greatest love—with eternal love;
- being with God in a covenantal relationship of mutual and reciprocal faith and trust, responsibility, and accountability;
- seeing the Face of God in every being, seeing the Divine in everyone and everything;
- the Divine in me acknowledging the Divine in you—Namaste;
- making the life of another as precious as our own;
- responding to hatred, anger, and, particularly, fear—with deep, unconditional, passionate, intense love;
- being in constant and extreme grace, kindness, caring, compassion, goodness, righteousness, generosity of spirit, decency, and dignity;
- giving our hands, resources, and hearts to repair and rejuvenate our world;
- consciously knowing and being continually aware that at the core of our being all is One. *One God—One World—One People*.

A world of unity can—and will—be built when we love radically, unconditionally, intensely, passionately.

A world of unity can—and will—be built out of the Radical Love of one human being for another and for God.

We *can* love God.

We *can* love each other.

We *can* love all humankind.

And the world can unfold into Love.

Through acts of love and loving kindness, we can affirm the best, the most thorough, the most passionate way to love:

With Radical Love.

With Greatest Love.

With Eternal Love.

BEING HOLY

And, how do we be Godlike?

Like God, we strive to be holy.

The sublime mandate rings through the millennia: "You shall be holy, for I, the Lord your God, Am holy" (Lev. 19:2).

To be holy means to be different, to be separate from any similar entity in the universe.

God is holy because God is unique from any other being.

We can be holy when we rise above the mundane; when we stand out from the ordinary; when we bring a sense of direction and purpose to our maddening world; when we care, share, and love.

We can be holy when we use our human power to think, reason, and remember—to feel the God-energy of Spirit flowing through us and inspiring our ideals and values.

We can be holy when we reflect God's ability to have relationships of unconditional love.

We can be holy when we heal our own brokenness so that we can join with God in the task of transforming and perfecting the world.

We can be holy when we feel the Divine Presence flowing within us, when our every thought, word, and deed make us God's partners here on Earth.

Holiness is:

In our sacred text, God tells us that when we own a piece of land—if we plant it, water it, weed it, and tend it with loving concern—when it comes time to harvest the crop, we are to leave the four corners of the field uncut (based on Lev. 19:9-10). Even though we are the current land owners, God is the ultimate LandLord, and God tells us—the corners do not belong to you. They belong to Me, and I give them to the poor, the hungry, and the needful in your midst.

No one need come to you for a handout, hoping that you had a good harvest, or that you are feeling charitable, or that you are big-hearted and generous, or that you need a tax deduction for your contribution. You are but the instrumentality to provide what is needed by another human being.

What you are doing is not, as your popular bumper sticker would have it, a "random act of kindness." It is an obligation, the sacred responsibility of human beings to take care of one another—a child of God making sure that all of God's other children live in dignity. The Bible's word for caring for another means "righteousness." It is the right, the fair, the just, thing to do.

God is far less interested in our religious rites and rituals than in how we behave as human beings, how we fulfill the Divine ethical mandate we have been given. In ancient times, the prophet Isaiah told us God's admonition:

> *This is the fast that I desire: To unlock the fetters of wickedness and to untie the cords of lawlessness; to let the oppressed go free; to break off every yoke. It is to share your bread with the hungry, and to take the wretched poor into your home. When you see the naked, clothe him, and do not ignore your own kin.* (Isa. 58:6)

At the core of God's instructions to us, the ways we are to behave with each other to elevate the human experience and the human spirit are the utterances known as the Ten Commandments.

An old legend says that, at Sinai, every soul that was created at the moment of creation—some in body on Earth, some in soul-form—came together for the theophoric moment of hearing God's word and will. The central moral teachings given to humankind are inherently engraved on each human soul.[1]

Based on the account of the Ten Commandments enjoined in

Exodus 20:1–17, a contemporary interpretation clarifies and expands upon God's imperative:

1. There is One God. Only One God. Singular. Unique. The One God created and continues to weave Godness throughout the universe and all humankind.

2. Each of us sees the One God's many facets and aspects in different ways, which celebrates our diversity in our unity. Yet we are warned to beware of the false gods that entice us—the gods that claim superiority over the One God; the gods that think they know better than the One God; the gods that deny the Oneness of God and God's universe; the gods that attempt to lure and deceive us.

3. With pure hearts, we can serve God in truth. Not our perversion of truth for our own purposes, but God's universal and eternal truth.

4. Be human. Work hard. Rest well. Play with abandon. Appreciate the world in which you live. Take the time to luxuriate in your contribution to the ongoing process of God's creation.

5. At the moment of conception, three are present—the mother, the father, and God. Parents are the caretakers and stewards of God's precious souls on Earth. Honoring parents is honoring God and celebrates the intrinsic Oneness of God and all of God's creatures.

6. Revere the sanctity of all life. Honor the interconnectedness of every human being.

7. Be faithful. Be honest and trustworthy. Be in integrity—in your most intimate relationship and with every other human being.

8. Cherish another's right to have and to keep.

9. Cherish another's good name and reputation.

10. Cherish your own self-worth, self-reliance, and self-satisfaction.

These injunctions have stood the test of time, because they encapsulate the human condition and the human experience. God, who created us and knows us intimately, insists that we strive for the highest level of holiness so that we elevate our human interaction and the human spirit.

Rather than being admonishments, these simple yet profound standards affirm the Oneness of God, God's human children, and God's world. Even one violation diminishes us all—while, during every moment we keep the Commandments, we happily journey toward righteousness and goodness.

God's continuing injunctions tell us how to treat every human being with decency and dignity:[2]

- Pay the day laborer wages at the end of each work day. Your worker may need the money to buy food.
- If you take a person's coat as pledge for a loan, return the coat at sundown. If the coat is the only collateral, the borrower may need it to stay warm that night.
- If you injure a person in a fight or an accident, pay for medical expenses and lost wages.
- In commerce, give fair weights and measures of the goods you sell.
- Your animals deserve thoughtful respect. When you plow your field, do not harness an ox and a donkey together. It can harm them both.
- Carefully watch the words that come out of your mouth. Gossip, false rumors, and slander have the power to pierce more deeply than the sharpest sword.

Deepening our commitment to being holy, we can offer the active works of our hands to help those who need our help; to lift up those who have been brought low; and to bring support, comfort, companionship, good cheer, and encouragement to all who crave human contact and assurance.

That is why almost every religious and faith tradition has its own, but very similar, version of what is known as The Golden Rule, which is as profound as it is simple: "Do unto others as you would have others do unto you."

We can make certain our society guarantees every human being—as a right, not a privilege—more than adequate food, shelter, and clothing; access to a superior education and outstanding health care; unfettered civil rights and human dignity.

We can care for the elderly, visit the sick, comfort the mourners, and provide for the widow and the orphan.

We can lend our voices and our votes to those who stand for honesty and integrity, justice and right action, compassion, and loving kindness.

We can work for a world free from tyranny and oppression; a world of equality, of freedom from fear and want; a world where the life of every person is safe and secure, respected, and cherished.

We can make sure that we give our children the gift of a world that will survive and flourish.

What the world so desperately needs right now is *Awesome Holiness*. Awesome Holiness is

- being constantly aware of the "Hereness" of God;
- bringing God into the world;
- being Godlike in thought, word, and deed;
- providing for the needs of the community;
- elevating and ennobling the human spirit;
- making the ordinary extraordinary;
- overcoming separation and celebrating Oneness;
- shaping the universe for good;
- working toward ultimate redemption for ourselves and our world.

Holiness is in each and every moment.
Holiness is in each and every person.
We can be Awesomely Holy.
And the world can be Holy with us.

BITTER-SWEET

What is stopping us from Radical Loving?

What is stopping us from Awesome Holiness?

What is stopping us from seeing the Face of God?

What is stopping us from seeing God in the face of every other human being?

What is stopping us from making the life of another as precious as our own?

What is stopping us from building a world of unity, of love, of Oneness?

Our own lives get in the way.

Sometimes life seems so wonderful. All we can think about is our own pleasure, our own gratification, our own success. We have little time or energy for anything else but our own self-serving feelings.

Sometimes we are bruised and battered by life's vagaries, life's randomness, or the pain and suffering that life brings to us and others. We have little time or energy for anything else except self-preservation.

Sometimes we feel as if we do not have control of our own lives. We are impeded by all the seemingly diverse forces in our lives that pull us in two opposite directions at the same time. We have a hard time balancing the many contradictions that swirl around us—our passions and our ambivalences, our high expectations, and our harsh realities.

We can be blinded by our own egos. We can be "puffed up" by our own perceived power. We can become "legends in our own minds." We are shocked when we discover that we are not masters of our domain and cannot bend the universe to our own will.

If we can get our egos and proclivities out of the way, we can remember that it is God—and God alone—who has set out the Divine Design for our lives.

And we know that God gives us a full measure of all that life has to offer—its tragedies and its triumphs, its deepest sorrows and its highest joys.

Surely, in our lives there is the bitter that corrodes our hearts and souls.

Yet there is the sweet and the good that we nourish and nurture.

Our task is to balance the evil and the good, the bitter and the sweet. As thinking, feeling human beings we can weave together stark differences and bring discernment and equilibrium to our lives.

> We discard the bitter rind of the pomegranate, the banana, the orange, and we eat of the sweetness of their fruits (inspired by BT Chagigah, 15b).
>
> We swallow the foul-tasting medicine, and we experience its healing powers.
>
> We place our bodies under the surgeon's sharp knife, and we are restored to health and well-being.
>
> We undergo the rigors of arduous, exhausting physical training, and we rejoice in our strength, vigor, and happy contentment.
>
> We tame the habits, behaviors, and addictions that plague us, and we feel the freedom and the relief from fear and need.
>
> We suffer the anguish of defeat, and we celebrate the jubilation of victory.
>
> We change dirty diapers and survive our children's "terrible twos" and the tender sensitivities of their adolescence and teenage years, and we watch with humility, gratitude, and deep satisfaction as they become awesome, magnificent human beings.

Out of turmoil, clarity can come.

Out of confusion, God can appear.

Out of seeming duality, melding and acceptance can arise.

Not "Either—Or."

"And."

"These AND these are the words of the Living God" (BT Eruvim, 13b).

SKY BLUE

Making Radical Loving and Awesome Holiness the guideposts and the patterns of our lives means that the mistakes or misdeeds we make with each other will seem more intense, more shameful and disgraceful, more consequential.

Can we recognize and admit our transgressions? Can we forgive ourselves? Can we seek forgiveness from those we have harmed? Will God ever forgive us?

When Moses came down the mountain with the set of tablets that contained God's instructions for our lives—what we commonly call the Ten Commandments—he saw that the people, in their lack of faith, had built an idol, a golden calf, to worship instead of worshipping God. In his frustration and fury, Moses smashed the holy tablets into tiny pieces (Exod. 32).

But God was not going to give up on us and called Moses up the mountain again. This time the people waited patiently, and when Moses returned with a second set of tablets, the people warmly accepted them.

From that time on, the Tablets of the Law were kept in the Holy Ark in the Tabernacle the people built for their desert sojourn. And, the people also reverently placed the shards from the first set of Tablets into the Ark. For the broken fragments were a stark reminder of disloyal faithlessness, yet still held the holiness of their original intent.

Today, for many of us, our lives feel broken and fragmented by the lack of faith, the discord and hatred that fills so much of our world.

Yet as it was for our desert-dwelling ancestors, we understand that there is holiness in the fragments and always, always, there is the promise of a "second chance," a way to repair and heal the brokenness and be whole once again.

The noted author, Rabbi Dr. Chaim Potok *zt"l*, taught (in the nonegalitarian language of his time), "The seeing of God is not like the seeing of man. Man only sees between the blinks. He does not know what the world is like during the blinks. He sees the world in pieces, in fragments. But God sees the world whole, unbroken. That world is good. Our seeing is broken. Can we make it like the world of God?"[1]

Dr. Heschel's theology answers, "God is not always silent, and man is not always blind. In every man's life, there are moments when there is a lifting of the veil at the horizon of the known, opening a sight of the eternal."[2]

That time is now—the time for the fulfillment of the ancient prophecy: "A time is coming when there will be a famine in the land; not a hunger for bread, nor a thirst for water, but for hearing the word of the Lord" (Amos 8:11).

God does not act alone; we are coequal partners in the quest. So God says, "When you call Me, and come and pray to Me, I will give heed to you. You will search for Me, and if only you seek Me wholeheartedly, you will find Me" (Jer. 29:12).

Humbly, and in eager anticipation we affirm in the words of our teacher, Rabbi Shlomo Carlebach *zt"l*:

> *You spoke to us once on Mt. Sinai,*
> *but the whole world did not hear You.*
> *So, we are asking You, Almighty,*
> *speak to us once again;*
> *let us hear Your Voice just once more.*
> *But, this time, let the whole world see it,*
> *and the whole world hear it.*
> *And we promise You*
> *that the whole world will know*
> *that You are there;*
> *that You are God.[3]*

We get a second chance!

We can bring Eden back to Earth.

We can live in bliss.

We can live in Paradise.

We can sit with God on the bench in the Garden and be in eternal love and holiness.

Most every religion and faith community has its own vision of the return to Eden. Many begin with the imagery of a person or an era that will herald and bring redemption, often called the Messiah or the Messianic Age.

Jews await the first coming of the Messiah, *Masheachvelt,* the World of the Messiah in *Masheachzeit,* the Time of the Messiah.

Christians believe that Jesus was the Messiah and long for His return in the Second Coming.

Muslims believe in the coming of *al-Masih.*

Buddhists expect *Maitreya* to arrive as the Messiah.

Hindus await the avatar of Lord Krishna.

Every religion and faith community holds the concept of a time when, through an individual person, or the unfolding into a particular era, the world will be enveloped in harmony and peace.

The irony is that, because the different religions have varying concepts about the Messiah, the very hope for a world of peaceful coexistence has been mired in disagreement and discord over (of all things) the idea of the Messiah!

If we were sitting on the park bench with God right now, we could very well imagine God saying, "Oh, My precious children, stop fighting with each other over something as silly as who or what the Messiah may be.

"You know very well that it is your hands that will plant the seeds, and it is your hearts that will nurture the growth of a world that is worthy of the Messiah.

"I will not simply plunk down the Messiah in your midst.

"When will the Messiah come? When you are ready—when you have healed the brokenness of your lives by building a world of justice, righteousness, and goodness. When you have brought, in the words of your Christmas song, 'Peace on Earth, good will toward men (and women).'

"Then the Messiah will come to announce and celebrate what *you* already have brought into being.

"And, My children, when the Messiah comes do not be complacent. You cannot simply sit around and luxuriate in an Earthly paradise. You must maintain what you have achieved.

"'If you are planting a tree, and someone tells you that the Messiah has come, first finish planting the tree and then go greet the Messiah.'[4]

"The Messianic Era is yours to create and sustain."

To take the concept of Messiah out of the "electrically charged" religious realms where controversy arises so often, here is a way to keep the idea and the hope and promise vitally alive while eliminating the differing language.

Do you remember playing hopscotch when you were young?

With chalk you drew a formation of numbered boxes on the sidewalk. The object of the game was to hop up those boxes numbered from one through nine to reach the far end.

Reach the top box, and you win! And do you remember what you called that very top box? Some people called it Ten, the last number in the sequence. Some people called it Goal. Some called it Home.

When I was growing up in Chicago, for some unknown reason we called it Sky Blue.

Sky Blue was our pinnacle of ultimate perfection.

The image of Sky Blue has stayed with me, and over the years it has become for me a symbol, a metaphor, for the ever-possible reality of the very best place we can be: a world of decency and dignity, justice and righteousness, goodness and peace, light and love. From a simple game from the innocent days of childhood comes an image that takes on powerful meaning. Sky Blue. A world of perfection.

If it were only as easy to bring a world of love, holiness, and peace as it is to play a little childhood game.

Maybe—just maybe—it is.

Presidents, prime ministers, and generals who make war are just grownup childhood game-players who sometimes forget:

Play by the rules.

Wait your turn.

Play nicely with others.

Don't run with scissors (or any other dangerous weapons) in your hand.

Play fair.

If you don't get your way, don't take your bat and ball and go home.

Don't be a bully.

Don't make anyone cry.

Stop the fighting back there, or someone is going to get hurt—and it's not going to be me.

Clean up after yourself; don't leave a mess.

Yes, you get graded for sportsmanship.

And if you don't behave well, it will go on your permanent record.

Sky Blue is the power and the promise of Eden on Earth once again. We simply need to be consciously aware and unequivocally committed to the reality that there is a world of Oneness.

Like our ancestors of old, despite the trials and tribulations we face, with perfect faith we believe in the coming of the Messiah.

We need to work every day to make it so.

We need to risk, for the reward is incredible. So: "Be bold. When you embark for strange places, don't leave any of yourself safely on the shore. Have the nerve to go into unexplored territory. You have to leave the city of your comfort and go into the wilderness of your intuition. What you discover will be wonderful. What you discover will be yourself."[5]

The Sky Blue of never-ending possibility fascinates and challenges.

The longings, and the energy, and the eagerness, and the love of our hearts, and our rejoicings, and our dreams, and our visions carry us to the long-awaited day.

Always, always—

Sky Blue awaits.

THE DAY IS DAWNING

What will embracing Radical Loving and Awesome Holiness mean for us and our world? What will striving to reach Sky Blue mean for our own hearts and souls?

According to the astronomical and astrological concept that divides time based on the movement of the Earth and the spring equinox, about six thousand years ago, when the history of humankind began—that is, when humankind became aware of and able to record its own place in the universe—the Earth, in relation to the Heavens, was aligned with the constellation Taurus the bull.[1] And in that pagan world, it was the bull that was the symbol of power, and for many, the symbol of the Divine.

In slow progression, two thousand years later the Earth moved into alignment with Aries, the sign of the ram. It was then that Judaism, with its ram of sacrifice and ram's horn, so central to its symbology, took center stage in the world.

Slowly, after another two thousand years, by the advent of Christianity, the Earth moved into alignment with Pisces, the sign of the fish, the symbol of Christianity to this day.

Now, two thousand years later, the Earth and Heavens have slowly moved once again. This time the Earth is moving into alignment with Aquarius, the water bearer—the symbol of cleansing, purification, rebirth, and renewal.

We now live at the "dawning of the Age of Aquarius," but not just as the sixties hippies, or the New Agers, or the Broadway musical, would have it.

It is the Age of Aquarius, the time for synthesis—for coming together and blending all the diverse elements that have divided us for so long—for the drawing of the pure water and the pure light that will wipe away the trash and the darkness that have plagued us for so long. It is time for the rebirth of the world.

The way into the Age of Aquarius for us and for our world is through the renewal of the World of Spirit, of the affirmation of the covenant of faith between God and each and every human being, of the intimacy and soul-connection that we can share with each other and with God.

It is a new birth-day for the world, and a new beginning for every one of us.

> Someday, after mastering the winds, the waves,
> the tides, and gravity we shall harness for God
> the energies of love, and then, for a second time in history
> we will have discovered fire.[2]

"I have plans that I have made for you, says God—plans for peace .... There *is* hope for your future" (Jer. 29:11).

> Return again.
> Return again.
> Return to the land of your Soul.
> Return to who you are.
> Return to what you are.
> Return to where you were born and reborn again.
> Return again.
> Return again.[3]

KNOWING BEYOND
KNOWING

With all that we do, with all that we accomplish to make our world a better place "out there," we need to journey to the "inside of our insides" to touch the deepest within us.

Our holy teacher, Reb Shlomo *zt"l* used to say to me, "You're the best. You're the sweetest and the holiest."

And then he would say to the next person, "You're the best. You're the sweetest and the holiest."

And he would say to the *next* person, "You're the best. You're the sweetest and the holiest."

And the next—and the next and the next. To each and every person he would say, "You're the best. You're the sweetest and the holiest."

Finally, someone asked him, "Reb Shlomo, how can this possibly be? If I am the best—if I'm the sweetest and the holiest—how can *she* be the best? How can *he* be the best? How can he be the sweetest and the holiest? How can she be the sweetest and the holiest? Isn't there only one best, one sweetest, one holiest?"

And Reb Shlomo would reply, "You *are* the sweetest, and you *are* the holiest, and you *are* the best."

And we all came to realize that Reb Shlomo was giving us a very deep teaching.

You, and you, and you, and you, *and I* ... are each and all the children of the Living God.

In each and every one of us is the best, the sweetest. In each and every one of us is the greatest holiness and unending love.

Yet sometimes we forget. We forget that "We are children of the Lord our God" (adaptation of Deut. 14:1).

Sometimes the vagaries and the vicissitudes of life beat us up or shove us down, and we begin to doubt our own goodness, our own worth. We let the outside world define who we are and how we measure our own value. We experience little satisfaction and feel less and less joy.

So we try to cover up our self-proclaimed deficiencies by making ourselves busy by going, going, going, and by doing—discovering, making, and working. We take little time to lead the Socratic "self-examined" life, or to shape our own identities and destinies.

Often, to defend or protect ourselves, we manifest anger, or bravado, or rigidity—or we fearfully build protective walls around our egos and lash out against anything or anyone we perceive to be threatening or harmful.

Truth be told, sometimes it may feel as if we are dead inside, as if we cannot get in touch with our true and deepest Self; that we cannot reach the "holy sparks" that never, ever go out.[1]

Yet everything we need to be the loving, holy person we want to be is within us.

> *A handful of wheat,*
> *five thousand years old,*
> *was found in the tomb*
> *of one of the kings*
> *of ancient Egypt.*
> *Someone planted the grains,*
> *and, to the amazement of all,*
> *the grains came to life.*

When we dig deeply within ourselves and touch the core of our beings, we know that no outside, external force can keep us from being the vessels of love that God created us to be. The holy sparks of God that are within us assure us that our hearts and souls know how to love.

God is Love. We are Love.

We know how to love our neighbor; we know how to love the stranger.

We know how to make the life of another precious and holy to us.

We know how to make this a better world.

When we send the love energy of our hearts out to the world, it zooms around the universe, entering every other heart. It impacts the whole planet, overcoming darkness and hatred, planting love in hardened hearts and increasing love in already-loving hearts. And the love we give out swirls back to us, and the circle of love ever-continues until it will envelop every place and every person.

> *A Native American tribe was known for its great ability to bring rain through its prayerful and joyful rain dances. Whenever this tribe was called upon to dance for rain, its members danced and danced, and it always rained.*
>
> *The Chief was asked, "How is it that even when all the other tribes fail, your tribe is so successful at bringing rain through your rain dances?"*
>
> *The Chief replied simply, "We just keep dancing until it rains."*

We can keep dancing until it rains.

We can love.

We can keep loving until, as ancient wisdom tells us, love "fills the Earth as the waters fill the sea" (Hab. 2:14).

We can keep loving until Oneness Consciousness fills every human being.

Awe is deep within us.

Wonder is all around us.

Imagination fills us.

Visions and dreams animate us.

Seeing is not just what is before us but what is in the darkness behind the blinking eye.

Hearing is not just listening to the words or the music but also to the silence in the pauses.

Knowing is not just comprehending the letters on the page but also in the white spaces between.

Perceiving is not just in the feeling but in the vastness of space and the infinity of ever-returning time.

We can come home to all we are, all we know, all we can be.

We can come Home to God.

We can come Home to our highest and very best Selves.

INNER JOURNEYS

We learn to love, we learn to be holy, by making the Inner Journey to touch the deepest parts of ourselves so that we can live in continuous God-energy. But that is not always an easy thing to do.

Sometimes God is right there sitting on the park bench, just waiting for us to come to talk. Yet often, we need to actively seek God.

The seeker's journey is to find the true meaning of life by finding God.

The British philosopher Aldous Huxley posited that there are four principles common to all spiritual pursuits:[1]

1. Everything is a manifestation of the Divine.
2. We can realize the existence of the Divine by intuition, which is superior to logic.
3. We have the capacity to identify with the Divine.
4. Human life has but one purpose—to identify with the Eternal Self, and thus, come into unitive knowledge of the Divine.

In simple practical terms, this means that we want to:

- find and know God.
- connect and communicate with God.
- live in the image of God by being God-like
- be God's partners in the ongoing creation of the universe

Even though God is Everything and Everywhere, and even though all we need to do is be consciously aware of God's Presence, the clamor, noise and distractions of this messy, material world we live in often make it very hard to find and embrace God.

"God," said the sage, "is everywhere you let God in."[2]

So how do we feel, touch, seek, come into loving intimacy with God?

My tradition teaches, "Say one hundred blessings a day."

St. Paul says, "Pray always."

Rebbe Nachman implores, "Pray, Pray, Pray."

One hundred blessings? Pray always?

We wouldn't have time to do anything else.

That, of course, is exactly the point.

If we say a blessing now and we know that we are going to say a blessing five minutes from now, we stay in continuous God-energy. We do not have time or opportunity to hate, cheat, or lie. We have time only to love—to love God and to love our fellow human beings.

There are myriad ways to come to God.

Each religion and faith community—and numerous other spiritual endeavors—give us pathways to the Divine: organized prayer, spontaneous prayer, meditation, text-study, and scholarly and popular literature; rituals, ceremonies, observances, celebrations, music, song, chanting, toning, and drumming; food, family, cultural, ethnic, geographic, and communal connections; dance, body-movement, and yoga; being in nature, sweat lodges, spiritual retreats, vision quests, and pilgrimages; the arts, stories, and legends; silence.

Yet no matter how involved we might be in these communal systems, finding and nurturing a relationship with God is deeply individual and personal.

Connecting and communicating with God can certainly take place in a communal setting, although we may find it difficult to be in intimacy with God while in a large group, instructed by a public leader, following a proscribed order. Perhaps we will find it better to be alone so that our personal encounter can be deeply intimate, so that we and God can be, in the words of Walt Whitman in *Leaves of Grass*, like "two of those cheerful waves rolling over each other and interwetting each other."

To begin to come into God-space and to engage in God-talk, we can use this simple image.

We turn Upward, Inward, and Outward.

Upward is just a metaphor. We know that God is Everywhere, yet the popular imagery of God sitting on a Heavenly Throne "up there" persists in our shared consciousness. So we ask: How do we get in touch with the transcendent God?

Just show up. Say: Here I Am. We can speak to God with our gratitude, our praise, our requests, our questions, our joys, our disappointments and anger, our awe, and our wonder.

And then—and this may be the hard part—we have to *listen* as God talks to us.

Turn *Inward*. Each person's relationship with God is so deeply personal that sometimes the only one who can be witness to you is you.

You can sense, feel, know, celebrate God.

You can sense, feel, know, celebrate yourSelf.

You can be brutally honest with yourSelf. Ask: Who Am I, and what is my life?

How do I celebrate all that is good in my life? How do I express gratitude for all that I have and hold dear? How do I express joy for this magnificent Earth where I live?

And, how do I heal my wounds and my pain? How do I repent my wrongs? How do I burn off any karma that plagues me? How do I best live God's plan for me? How do I fulfill my life-mission? How can I be a better human being tomorrow than I am today?

And, then turn *Outward*. We can give our hearts and the works of our hands to healing this broken world in which we live. We can truly be God's partners on Earth.

We can: feed the hungry, shelter the homeless, bring healing to the ill, educate the illiterate, comfort the disturbed, protect the most vulnerable, give voice to the voiceless, give hope to the hopeless.

To the dark places, we can bring light. To the tumultuous places, we can bring calm and tranquility. To the places of conflict, we can bring harmony. To the places of hatred, we can bring love. To the places of warfare, we can bring peace.

Wherever and whenever our meeting with the Divine takes place—whether it be in a large gathering or in private solitude—to facilitate our conversation with God, it is helpful to have a set of "Mystical Spiritual Tools" that have been time-tested and true to enable and enhance the experience.[3]

DO NOT FEAR

Since God is Everything and is in Everything, we may find it intimidating, overwhelming, and even frightening to intentionally come into God's Holy Presence—to be in personal connection and communication with the Creator, Sustainer, Commander, and Redeemer of the universe. Rather, it can be the most joyful of all human experiences, for being with God means being totally enveloped, totally infused with God's grace and love. Talking with God is like the sweetest pillow talk of the most ardent lovers. Being in conversation with God is wondrous and awesome. When we embrace the moment with courage and strength, we embrace God.

SPIRITUAL INTENT

While some can come to God through the intellect, most find the pathway to the Divine by coming through the World of Spirit. When we open our hearts and souls, we remember God's Heart and Soul. Here, too, it can be intimidating, for letting go of the protective armor of our egos can make us very vulnerable. Yet when we set our Intention to find God through the emotional and spiritual aspects of our human Beingness, we can seek the sacred. We can know that there is only Oneness with God and with the universe. We can be the Oneness.

SILENCE

In the onslaught of noise that fills our world we can find a quiet place to still our mouths, our minds, and our souls. In the sound of silence we can find our voices. We can look deep within to find our concerns, passions, questions, needs, and desires. In the darkness of silence, we can plant and grow the new creation that leads to our enlightenment.

MERGE AND FLOW

Even though it can be difficult to surrender and not be in control, in the most intimate way, we can cleave into God's Being; we blend, meld, merge. We come into alignment, attunement, At-Onement with God. We come into God's energy field, get onto God's wavelength, enter into God's Light-sphere. We come into the deepest I-Thou relationship with the Eternal Thou.[4]

ISOLATION

Sometimes it can be frightening to be alone with our own thoughts, our own doubts, our own fears—but we *can* go into both the deepest and the highest places within ourselves. We can go to the place within us beyond identity, character, and disposition. We can go even further than self-isolation—meaning being alone in reflection, introspection, discernment, and self-evaluation. We can go to isolation from Self, the burning of our ego.

SELF-UNDERSTANDING

We can delve into our psyches and souls. We can come to understand what motivates us, what drives us. We can strive to understand our hungers, our passions. We can examine why we are, who we are, what we are. We can ask that a measure of God's positive attributes be reflected in us.

BE IN ECSTASY

What a great gift life is! How fortunate we are to be alive at this moment in time. How happy we are to be part of this great adventure on Earth. We can come to God in gladness. We can: manifest joy—sing gratitude—dance in exaltation—praise God in exhilaration—be in bliss.

LISTEN

Conversation with God has two parts: We talk, God listens. God talks, we listen. Listen. Listen. Listen. We can hear God—gather in what God wants us to know, to feel, to experience, to do. We can be the vessel that is filled with God's Light and God's Love. Like Moses coming down the mountain, we can let God shine and beam through us. We can let God come through us to bless the work of our hands and through us to give the world guidance and direction.

Even when acquiring these powerful Mystical Tools with which to come to God, we are still a people in a hurry. We want to be in intimate relationship with the Divine, but all too often our fast-paced, technologically-driven lives leave us little time to think, feel, contemplate, meditate, and pray.

So, here are four very short meditations/prayers that we can say "On The Go," when we want to connect and communicate with God.[5]

    🙰 Sometimes, there are no words. There is only connection at the deepest, deepest level. It is then that we find God in silence.

> *Be still.*
> *And know*
> *that I Am God.*

➤ Sometimes, our prayer can be our response to the incredible mysteries, wonders, and adventures of living life with its all tragedies, and its triumphs and never-ending surprises.

Hello God. WOW!

➤ Sometimes, our prayer can be a declaration of our union with God and God's Divine Design.

Here I Am.
I Am Ready to Listen to Your Word and Do Your Will.
Purify my heart to serve You in Truth.
Use me.

➤ Sometimes, we have only a few seconds to communicate with God. My dear friend, Father James J. O'Leary, S. J. (you'll meet him in an upcoming chapter) gives us this simple, yet deep, heartfelt prayer. Perhaps, these words are all we will ever need, for in even the briefest moment of encounter there is all of Creation.

I love You.
I'm sorry.
Please help me.
Thank You.

In prayer and meditation, we can expand into the Divine.
We can give God our hearts.
We can be One with God.
We can come back to God over and over again.
And God will say, "Here is your place with Me (Exod. 33:21).
"Come into My heart, My precious children.
"We will know each other in love.
"I will hold you close.
"Your soul will be content, and you will be happy."

LINEAGE AND LEGACY

How do we learn to love?
By being loved. And emulating love.
How do we learn to be holy?
By experiencing holiness. And emulating holiness.

Going back only ten generations, each of us has 1,024 direct ancestors. Each of those 1,024 people left a lineage and a personal legacy. If any of them had lived in a different place, received a different education, married a different person, parented in a different way, gotten in the way of a different political or social movement, been involved in a different war or peace, then everything—*everything*—would be different.

We know that genetic traits can be passed through the generations. Our children can bear a striking physical resemblance to our great-great-grandparents. Physical strengths and weaknesses are often duplicated generation to generation. A proclivity toward certain types of work—athletics and the arts, for example—seems to be within certain families. And sadly, for some there seems to be a history of diseases that run in the family, and physical and mental illnesses that manifest time and again.

We are happy when grandsons have Grandma's beautiful blue eyes. And we are proud when our granddaughters have the inherent skills to follow into the family business. And we rejoice that modern medical science and advanced technology are working tirelessly to master the faulty DNA that causes ongoing pain and suffering.

Yet there are still some inherited dispositions that remain puzzling and troubling. Distrust, despair, anger, fear, insecurity, anguish, loss, grief, and guilt are felt and manifest in many lives. They are present in so many lives; they cause real personal pain and affect all those who come in contact with the sufferer. From where do these woundings come—how can they be understood—and how can they be healed?[1]

Throughout the generations, so many people have been exposed to great trauma—war, death, destruction, rape, subjugation, pillage, plunder. Harsh and ruthless voices have shouted cruel and frightening threats. Innocent souls have been tormented and mercilessly abused. Brutal killers have slashed their ways through towns, and villages, and bodies. Beatings, imprisonments, torture, holy wars, crusades, pogroms, genocide. Holocaust. Debasement. Terror. Horror.

How does a human body—with its eternal soul—respond to all this affront, all this abomination?

Modern science affirms that there is an inextricable body-mind connection.[2] Words, good or evil, spoken to water or to plants change the chemical composition. People who are ill for whom prayers are said—whether or not they are aware of the prayers—heal more rapidly than those for whom no prayers are recited.

In the same way, severe trauma gets recorded at the deepest level—in the soul and in the genetic makeup of the DNA. Epigeneticists tell us that severe trauma can cause a mutation in the genes. That mutation is passed on to future generations through the DNA and becomes a part of the DNA structure. Much of our human DNA is made up of layers of trauma mutation.

New babies are born with the mutated genes of their lineages, and from the very beginning, come into this world with the pain of terror and trauma in their beings, just as surely as they come in genetically with blue eyes or red hair. These mutations can negatively affect a person throughout an entire lifetime. And they may then be played out on life's larger stage as we understandably become defensive and protective when perceiving a real or imagined threat.

It is time for the lineages to be healed. It is time to break the cycle of broken DNA being passed from generation to generation. It is time for individuals to be rid of inherited pain. It is time for the world to no longer have to fear the actions of those who lash out in unrecognized, but nevertheless real affliction.

If we sense that our lineage needs healing, we can begin to restore the love and holiness that may have been stifled or lost in the trauma-pain of the generations.

Contemporary spiritual seekers, Jonah and Rebecca Balogh, offer this Lineage Process for those who wish to heal:

Stand with your hands at your sides, palms facing forward, and say:

> *I now have 100 percent desire*
> *that all my lineages be cleared*
> *of all pain and all suffering*
> *so that I grow in perfect harmony with Full Grace.*
> *Let there be perfect integrity in all my being,*
> *in all my souls, in all my lineages, in all my heart*
> *for the purpose of healing all lineages*
> *so that the fullness of life is now realized.*
> *We now have 100 percent desire*
> *that all lineages are now clear*
> *so that they hold the Original Beauty*
> *of the Great Love.*

Who are we?
What are our lives?
We are Then.
We are Now.
We can be Who We Can Be.
    Loved and Loving.
    Whole and Holy.

A PAINFUL TRUTH

Even with our fondest hopes and fervent desires, even with our most Radical Loving and Awesome Holiness, sometimes—many times—wholeness can be elusive. Differences are sharp and stark; reconciliation and healing cannot come to be.

In places where hatred is so great and strong, where intervention is futile, then sometimes the fires of loathing have to burn themselves out by themselves.

In places where the darkness is so dense and deep, it seems that light cannot possibly penetrate.

In places in our own lives where abuse, betrayal, broken trust, violation, or abandonment has been so hurtful and painful, then resolution may never come.

Words and acts against us may be totally deplorable and inexcusable. Some people may be too toxic for us; some may break our hearts and crush our spirits. Tragically, sometimes people and places are unredeemable.

Yet we cannot allow anyone or any memory to drag us down or hold us back. Sometimes it is best to cut all ties and walk away from whatever and whomever has appalled and aggrieved us. And, as antithetical as that may seem to our quest for unity and harmony, it is perfectly all right. For we are breaking free from ties that bind, protecting our psyches, and reclaiming our own power.

Still, the reality of pain, the oft-perceived stigma, the ongoing personal and societal reverberations, and the burden of memory may feel as if they are too much to bear.

As hard as it is to imagine, perhaps the way to our own solace and tranquility is to forgive. We do not have to carry the hurt, the pain. We do not have to wallow in the wrongs done to us and the prisons that our own minds may create for us.

"Forgive" means "to give back." We can return our soul-burden to its source by offering compassion, absolution, exoneration to the one who has harmed us.

We can always hope for penance and atonement from our perpetrator. And even if it is not offered, we can experience release from our anguish, and redemption from our travail, because we are choosing to let go of what holds and binds us.

Yes, the nobility of human forgiveness can be offered in this Earthworld. But as much as we may wish and we may try, sometimes forgiveness is just not ours to give. The offender is too evil. The pain is too great. The repercussions are too massive.

Happily, there is a higher and more effective pathway to forgiveness. For ultimately, granting forgiveness belongs to God. It is up to God to forgive those who have harmed us. And it is up to God to accept our inability to forgive.

When we cannot hold the pain any longer, we can give it to the One with the big enough shoulders and heart to take on all our horrors, agony, and tears. God is ready to receive whatever we need to give away, whatever will unburden us.

We need not rationalize, or pretend, or forget—but there are times when it is best, as difficult as it may be and as significant as the ripple of consequences may become—to let go and give away to God whatever torments us. With God's help, we need never be hapless victims. We can always be triumphant survivors who sever ourselves from our suffering and sorrow and find a modicum of peace.

If we break off relationships with those who harm us, what does that mean for our quest for wholeness, for Oneness?

We know we can have wide differences—as abhorrent as some of those differences may be to us—as long as we remain civil, respectful, and nonviolent. This surely does not mean that we will sit quietly by and simply accept intimidation or coercion thrust upon us, or continue to accept the abominations that are perpetrated upon us, or the evils and ills that beset our world. And we will not countenance harm or defilement done to any one of us.

Instead, we can be Light and Love. We can champion and embrace the compass of morality, and we can call the world to goodness and righteousness. We can work to weave together disparate and contentious pieces into a loving and holy whole. As the Kotzker Rebbe taught, "There is nothing more whole than a broken heart."

A monkey in a tree hurled a coconut at the head of a traveler.

The traveler picked up the coconut, drank its refreshing milk, ate its sweet flesh, and made a bowl from its sturdy shell.

And the traveler continued on the journey.

BEING IN AWE

The twins, love and holiness, have twin siblings—awe and gratitude.

Rabbi Dr. Abraham Joshua Heschel *zt"l* taught us: "Awe is a sense for the transcendence ... to the mystery beyond all things ... an act of insight into a meaning greater than ourselves. It enables us to perceive in the world intimations of the Divine ... to sense in small things the beginnings of infinite significance .... Awe is a way of being in rapport with the mystery of all reality ... to live life in radical amazement."

If only we are consciously aware, then each new breath—each morning's awakening, each thought, each feeling—can invoke a sense of awe.

If only we are consciously aware, then each glance—at the sun that lights our days and the moon and stars that illumine our nights; at the ground on which we walk; at the forests, mountains, and canyons that humble us; at the seas that surround us; at the cool breezes that refresh us; at the rains and dew that sustain us; at each vision of stunning beauty—can invoke a sense of awe.

If only we are consciously aware, then each moment of existence made for us to revel in its glory—pregnant with possibility; given in anticipation of the next; of wonder and amazement—can invoke a sense of awe.

If only we are consciously aware, if we can feel our connection to All That Is, to the creation and re-creation of our place and purpose, to the One who is the Source of All, to the mysteries and magic of the cosmos—we can invoke a sense of awe.

Everything is in the hands of God, except the awe of God.[1]

In God's Holy Presence We Are in Awe!

BEING IN GRATITUDE
AND JOY

For the astonishing and awesome universe we witness every moment, we can be in nothing less than the deepest thanksgiving and immense gratitude. We recognize our good fortune; we celebrate what our eyes see, our ears hear, our hearts feel. We are grateful beyond measure. We say, "Thank You" for all that we are and all that we have.

We can begin with a grateful heart:

> *Every morning, my first conscious thought is I am breathing. I am alive. The Breath of God, the Presence of God, flows through me. So in overwhelming gratitude I speak words from my tradition: "I am grateful to You, living and eternal Sovereign, for in Your great compassion and faithfulness You have restored my soul to me."*

We can be grateful for our physical well-being:

> *I praise You and thank You, O God, that I and the ones I love are healthy and well; that I have food to eat, a place to live, and clothes to wear; that today I was saved from illness, accident, and harm; that no evil has befallen me and no pain has engulfed me.*

And we can be grateful for our spiritual calling.

> *I praise You and we thank You, O God, for setting me in the beauty of creation; for instilling in me the breath of life; for choosing me to be Your partner; for endowing me with the capacity to think, reason, remember, and the potential to create, grow, and*

choose; for teaching me the difference between right and wrong; for granting me the discernment to temper justice with compassion; for enabling me to feel success and joy, failure and pain; for giving me the extraordinary power to care, share, love, and bring healing and hope; for calling and challenging me to be human and humane, to do well and do good.

We can offer continual gratitude:

There is magic and miracles in the words "Thank you." We can thank our spouses, our children, our parents, our siblings, our friends, our co-workers, and the members of our community for all they are to us and all they mean to us.

We can express unending gratitude for Divine guidance and protection:

We can say,

> *If troubles come my way,*
> *if sickness overtakes me,*
> *if I experience pain and anguish,*
> *if evil people try to destroy me,*
> *it is they, my enemies and foes,*
> *who stumble and fall.*
> *If an army would besiege me,*
> *my heart would not fear.*
> *If war were waged against me,*
> *even if my father and mother forsook me,*
> *I would still be confident ...*
> *because*
> *You, O God are the stronghold of my life.*
> *You, O God are my light and my salvation.*
> *You, O God will take care of me* (adaptation of Ps. 27).

When we stay connected to God and in constant gratitude to God, no matter what happens to us—at the pinnacles of our greatest happiness or in the depths of our wild despair—together with God we can do anything and everything.

I thank You, God. I thank You, God.

We can express gratitude for all the gifts and the blessings we have been given and all we continue to receive:

> For the blessings which You lavish upon us in forest and sea,
> in mountain and meadow, in rain and sun, we thank You.
> For the blessings You implant within us,
> joy and peace, meditation, and laughter,
> we are grateful to You.
> For the blessings of friendship and love,
> of family and community,
> For the blessings we ask of You and those we cannot ask,
> For the blessings You bestow upon us openly,
> and for those You give us in secret,
> For the blessings we recognize,
> and for those we fail to recognize,
> For the blessings of our tradition
> of memory, and vision, and hope,
> For all these blessings which surround us on every side,
> Dear God, hear our thanks and accept our gratitude.[1]

It takes a gracious, open-hearted, genuine person to be able to say, "Thank you. I appreciate you. I am grateful to you." It takes a humble person to know that he or she must.

I have found a very effective way to be in daily love and gratitude to those who have shaped my life.

I remember that I have 1,024 direct ancestors who came before me and formed the foundation of my life, and those who were my loving companions in this lifetime who have gone on to the Great Beyond.

All of us can give thanks and express everlasting gratitude to our ancient ancestors and to our own grandparents, mothers and fathers, sisters and brothers, sons and daughters, wives and husbands and partners, life-beloveds, and closest friends—those most dear to us.

They are surely entwined with our souls, and tug at our hearts, and perch on our shoulders—and we gently and lovingly wrap them in our love. Our prayers bid us: "Remember the covenantal love, the loving kindness, of your ancestors."

We can still hear their voices; we can feel their warm embrace; we can sense their hopes, dreams, and aspirations; we can recognize their character; we can know their love.

And we can express our gratitude to our life-companions, to all with whom we live and learn, grow, and celebrate.

I have compiled for myself a rather lengthy personal list of the people (both those gone from this Earth and those blessedly present in my every day) who have deeply touched my life and influenced me for good.

At the very beginning of this list I name my precious ancestors who have passed from this Earthly world.

Then I enumerate my Spirit Guides, the souls from The Other Side who have chosen to help me in my life and my work.

The list continues with my teachers from antiquity on—the wise and wonderful sages, rebbes, and guides whose writings and teachings have most shaped my thinking and my spirit.

Then there is the list of all the personal teachers from whom I have learned so much—from my early youth until this very day—and the colleagues with whom I continue to study and learn.

The list goes on to include my dearest family and closest friends who have and who continue to share this life-journey with me—who influence me with their ideas and evolving thinking, and their friendship and love.

Finally, the list contains the names of a few of my special students, for "I have learned much from my teachers, even more from my colleagues, but from my students, I have learned the most" (BT Berachot, 7a).

Each day, before I begin my prayers and meditations with God, I read this list to myself, and I am in awe and gratitude for all that has been given to me. I remember from where I come, how I got where I am, and who will continue to be with me on my journey.

In unending gratitude and love, I pay tribute to them. And I ask what each has to teach me that day—what insight, assistance, guidance, and inspiration I might receive by remembering what they have already given me, and by hearing or intuiting what they may still have to give at this particular moment.

Each of us can be grateful for our origins, our lineage, our formation, our connections, and our destinies. I humbly and happily recommend this spiritual practice.

*

Being in Awe and Gratitude leads to being Joyful and Happy. The Bratslaver taught, "It is a big/important commandment [exemplary behavior] to always be happy."

Even in the midst of the destitute conditions in which she worked, the sainted Mother Teresa taught us, "The best way to show gratitude to God is to accept everything with joy."

She was reflecting the Scripture she had learned as a child and lived all her life: "Serve God with gladness. Come before God with songs of joy" (Ps. 100:2).

The concept of joy has so many levels and layers that it takes many words to convey all the subtitles. A more than two hundred-year-old prescription for happiness is as relevant now as it was then:

> *Nine requisites for contented living:*
> *Health enough to make work a pleasure.*
> *Wealth enough to support your needs.*
> *Strength enough to battle with difficulties and overcome them.*
> *Grace enough to confess your sins and forsake them.*
> *Patience enough to toil until some good is accomplished.*
> *Charity enough to see some good in your neighbor.*

Love enough to move you to be useful and helpful to others.
Faith enough to make real the things of God.
Hope enough to remove all anxious fears concerning the
future.[2]

We can learn how to feel joy because: "To live happily is an inward power of the soul."[3]

When we are in joy, we can find our inner bliss: "Joy is the echo of God's life within us."[4] When we know God, we know joy.

Our morning prayer affirms our delight at being God's children on Earth, and delighting in the gifts God gives us.

Happy are we.
How good is our portion.
How fine is our lot in life.
How sweet is our inheritance.
How delighted are we
that each day we proclaim
The Oneness of God,
The Oneness of the Universe,
The Oneness of All That Is.
Rejoice!

BEING IN THE GARDEN

We rejoice at the grandeur of this Earth that God has given us—the stunning beauty of the blue sky and the fluffy white clouds, the seas and the mountains, the forests and the deserts, the canyons and the plains.

In the midst of all this beauty our soul-memories have glimmers of the original Garden, the Paradise of Eden on Earth. So as often as we can, we go out into the great outdoors to refresh and rejuvenate our souls and our relationship with our Creator God.

In Scripture, literature, and poetry the Garden is often a metaphor for God. Coming into the Garden is coming into God's Light and Love. That is why the Rebbe-sage Nachman of Bratslav so reveled in being in the splendor of nature.

May it be my custom to go outdoors each day
among the trees and grass—among all growing things
and there may I be alone, and enter into prayer,
to talk to the One to whom I belong.
May I express everything in my heart
and may all the foliage of the field—
all the grasses, trees, and plants—
awake at my coming,
to send the powers of their life into the words of my prayer
so that my prayer and speech are made whole
through the life and spirit of all growing things
which are made as One by their transcendent Source.

We can remember what the Angels said to God when God declared that the crowning act of creation was going to be human beings. They told God not to create humankind, for the Angels feared that we human beings would deface and destroy the wondrous works of creation that God had just made. Yet God went ahead and created humankind, but not without a word of caution:

> *When God created the first human beings,*
> *God led them around all the trees of the Garden*
> *of Eden, and said, "Look at My works! See how*
> *beautiful they are—how excellent. For your sake*
> *I created them all. See to it that you do not spoil and*
> *destroy My world, for if you do, there will be no one*
> *to repair it."* (Midrash Kohelet Rabbah 1 on Eccles. 7:13)

We know that the very best way to live in this world, to be in holy love, to be in continual awe and gratitude and joy, is to feel comfortable and safe in our place. We need to know that—literally and figuratively—we stand on solid ground, that we are well protected from any danger that may come our way, and that we are wise enough to make the good choices that sustain and strengthen our existence.

Yet at this moment our lives and the very existence of this precious planet are in imminent danger. Good science tells us Climate Change on this Earth is very real and poses an immediate existential threat to the very existence of our planet.

Certainly, ongoing cycles of nature are partly responsible—as they have been since the beginning of time. But there can be no argument that the actions of human beings have tremendous additional effect on the delicate balance that Earth needs in order to survive.

When we human beings pollute the skies and the waters—when we strip the land of its minerals, denude the forests of their trees, and bombard the ozone layer with our sprays—we diminish the health of our planet. And when we soak the lands with the blood of our wars of hatred, the very soil cries out in pain.

What happens in one place affects what happens everywhere. Smoke that a chimney belches in Pittsburgh pollutes the skies of London. Carbon emissions in Paris darken the skies of Russia. Oil spills from the coast of Japan wash up on the shores of San Francisco. One plastic bottle thoughtlessly tossed into a lake or stream floats its way into the belly of a fish, haplessly killing it and affecting the entire ecosystem.

When we are careful and respectful, we can enhance the condition and vitality of the place where we live. We can protect our lands, skies, and seas so that we, and generation after generation, can enjoy them and derive the greatest pleasure and benefit from them.

When we restore Eden on Earth, we do not want to have to go around picking up the trash and separating the recyclables. We want to be able to luxuriate in the natural beauty that God gave us. We are holy beings when we maintain the beauty, the grandeur, the sacred-ness of the glorious planet that is our home. "The Heavens are God's, but the Earth, God has given to humankind" (Ps. 115:16). We want to sit on the Garden's bench with God, proud that we have been good stewards and caretakers of the precious Earth that we have been given.

Surely, governments and international organizations bear great responsibility in saving our planet from self-destruction. Yet the task belongs to each and every individual.

An old story:

> *A man in a boat began to drill a hole under his seat.*
> *His fellow passengers protested. "What concern is it of yours?"*
> *he responded. "I am making the hole under my seat, not yours."*
> *They replied, "That is so, but when the water comes in, it will*
> *sink the whole boat and we will all drown."[1]*

We call on governments of all nations to take immediate and thor-ough steps to lead their citizenry—individuals and businesses and all government agencies—to safeguard the Earth. We call on the United States of America to swiftly rejoin the Paris Climate Agreement and to strengthen the powers and the funding of the Environmental Protection Agency (EPA). And we call on every human being on this planet to take a proactive part in the ongoing processes of protecting and restoring the environment.

For each of us, it is not hard. We have been given simple yet very effective ways to help save the planet. Use less water, electricity, paper, fossil fuel. Recycle plastic, paper, electronics, rubber, oil, unused medications. Take garbage to dump. Reuse grocery bags and liquid containers. Do not throw trash onto the streets, or old junk into the waterways, or bombard the atmosphere with the pollutants from hair-sprays. Do not drive when you can walk, print when you can write, or buy when you might borrow. Eat sustainable foods. Plant a tree to add oxygen to the air.

Lest we forget or ignore our sacred task of caring for this precious Earth, we are proud to see that our children are now rising up in a worldwide movement to remind us. For they know the truth of the old Pueblo tribal teaching: "I did not inherit this Earth from my parents. I am borrowing it from my grandchildren."

When we love the Earth, we love God and we love God's creation. We love our role in protecting Earth, and we love the happy task of giving our children and generations yet unborn the great gift of a beautiful, grand, glorious home in which to live.

> *"We are One.*
> *We join with the Earth and with each other*
> *for the healing of our planet and the renewal of all life."*[2]

Once we begin acting as if we are in the Garden of Eden on Earth— we are!

BEING HUMAN

When I was a little boy, whenever I went outside to be with my friends my mother or father would call out to me, "Play nice out there."

These days it seems as if no one is playing nice out there. Our world has become a swamp of mean and nasty behavior and uncivil, rude discourse. Not only are nations pitted against each other, but racial, gender, class, and cultural warfare seems to be the new norm in far too many places.

Where is the love? Where is the holiness? Where is the awe? Where is the gratitude? Where is the joy?

It is difficult and discouraging to see the love and holiness in each human being trampled by humiliating, shameful—and often highly prejudicial—acts of self-proclaimed self-righteousness.

There are myriad places and situations where rigidity and inflexibility and resolute preconceptions prevail over cooperation, compromise, reconciliation, and resolution.

As complicated and complex as are the theological, ethnic, racial, national, gender, cultural, sociological, and social reasons that drive the incivility in our world today, it can all be addressed in one mandate that can solve so much of what plagues us: Don't be a bully!

Bullying is using position and power to force, coerce, intimidate, abuse, or threaten another. It can be physical or verbal, emotional or spiritual, explicit or implied. It can take place anywhere: on the international stage, in the halls of government, in the community, in the marketplace, in academia, in the home, in the schoolyard. And, in this technological age, bullying can be cyber.

Anybody can be a bully: a president of a country, a workplace boss, a military or peace officer, a sexual predator, a spouse or partner, a parent, a teacher or coach, a counselor, a teenager, or a five-year-old.

Bullying means that love is supplanted by contempt, holiness is diminished, and the human spirit is dimmed—both for the one who is bullied, and, realize it or not, for the one who bullies.

Just listen to our world for a moment:

> Where have respect and good manners gone?
>
> Why do we scream and yell at each other?
>
> Why do so many have an attitude of superiority, a sense of entitlement?
>
> How did our public discourse become so dogmatic, narrow-minded, polarized, mean-spirited, and shrill?
>
> How have great political debates devolved into such rigid partisan positions?
>
> Why do people in power continue to exploit the weak and vulnerable?
>
> Why is there still such discrimination against people of color, LGBTQs, immigrants, and those who are "different"?
>
> Why is there still so much sexual harassment of and so much inequality for women?
>
> How have gangs, drugs, and violence taken over our streets?
>
> How do we countenance racial profiling and police shootings?
>
> Why are our roads full of rage?
>
> How has our human condition so deteriorated that we get into fist fights on airplanes, supermarket checkout lines, and at children's sports games?
>
> Why do bullets still tear through our schools, workplaces, movie theaters, and places of worship?
>
> How have we let the internet become an instrument of falsehood, and intimidation and fear?

How has childhood teasing devolved into wicked traumatizing?

The sad answer to our questions is that we often feel so belittled by others that we have to demonstrate our own power. When we feel that we are brought low, we have to rise up; we have to overcome. Whether we are a president, a boss, or a child on the playground—we have to feel stronger and better than everyone else.

Be clear. This is not about another's weaknesses or faults; it is about our own need to justify ourselves to ourselves, to bolster our own self-esteem. We evoke grandiosity and power to make ourselves feel good. We put down another in order to build ourselves up.

That's not love; that's not holiness.

We need to restore civility to our world. We need to assure decency and dignity for every person on the face of this Earth.

We begin with *our words* because they carry so much power.

No more rudeness. No more lack of courtesy, politeness, or good manners. No more taunting and teasing. No more road rage. No more workplace intimidation. No more sexual harassment. No more trash talk. No more crudeness and lewdness. No more spewing hostility and hatred. This kind of talk is the symptom of egocentric, narcissistic, self-centered attitudes and behavior. It diminishes and crushes the human spirit and it rips at the fabric of a civilized society.

It is time to restore decorum and decency to our words with and about each other.

We can just stop speaking negative and offensive words. Instead, we can say: "Let the words of my mouth and the meditations of my heart be acceptable to You, O God" (Ps. 19:14). If our words are worthy enough for God, they will be proper enough for our fellow human beings.

And we can embrace the dignity of each and every human being.

We can, for example, not talk of "the poor" and "the needy," but we can speak of those who are at this moment in time *needing*. A subtle difference to be sure, but our words create a mindset—both for the speaker and the listener.

And we can reframe how we perceive each other. Citizens need no longer see law enforcement officers as enemies to be feared and avoided. And the police need no longer racially profile and unduly accuse. Our law enforcement officers must truly serve and protect us.

And we cannot discriminate against any human being for any reason, because we are all, each and every one of us, a child of God—perfect and totally equal in God's eyes.

> *A sophisticated city dweller was sitting in the lobby of a fancy hotel. Sitting next to him was a Native American, a Tribal Elder in full ceremonial dress.*
>
> *The city dweller stared at the Elder for a long moment, and then he could no longer contain his curiosity. "Excuse me. I can't help but notice your costume. Are you really a full-blooded Native American?"*
>
> *"Well, no," replied the Elder thoughtfully. "I am short one pint that I gave to save a white man's life."*

Ban Ki-moon, Secretary General of the United Nations, spoke poignantly of human rights. He was speaking specifically about the LGBTQ community, but his words apply to all human beings:

> *Every year, hundreds are killed, thousands are badly hurt and millions live their lives under the shadow of discrimination and disapproval. That is an outrage.*
>
> *I ask those who use religious or cultural arguments to deprive ... people of their rights: What do you gain by making others less equal? Is your religious culture so weak that the only way you can sustain it is by denying others basic rights?*[1]

The pathway to a revival of good taste and goodness is stark and serious, yet it can be very, very simple.

We can stop exploiting others.

We can stop crushing the human spirit.

We can be sweet.

We can be holy.

We can be love.

BRAIDING

A world of love and holiness, a world that inspires awe, gratitude, and joy begins in the most intimate relationships.

In the beginning, when the Tree of Life and of the Tree of Knowledge of Good and Evil split, the Divine Masculine and the Divine Feminine separated from each other.

That separation is mirrored in our human relationships here on Earth. Throughout our sojourn on this Earth, far beyond different biological and physical characteristics, there has been a stark male-female division/separation. With obvious exceptions, historically, men and women most often have had different roles, different life-views, different priorities. And surely, men have most often held and used the authority and power in the public arena and, as most men have perceived it, in personal relationships and at home.

As one writer satirically and sardonically put it, "Men are from Mars; Women are from Venus." Or, as another describes it, men and women speak *In a Different Voice*.[1]

In order for the world to have any chance to return to the Oneness of Eden, the original breech between the masculine and the feminine—played out throughout the millennia—must be healed.

This is no easy task, for in the beginning Oneness was a providential gift of grace from the Divine. Our progenitors forfeited that precious gift, and humankind has suffered the repercussions and the consequences ever since.

Our task, critical and immediate, is to grow in Oneness Consciousness—and surely in partnership with the Divine, who provides guidance and direction—to bring back Eden through our own works.

We can once more be in perfect alignment with Full Source.

Separation can end.

Exile can end.

The Divine Feminine, Shechinah, and the Divine Masculine, Source, can be united in Oneness. The Tree of Knowledge of Good and Evil can stand upright and braid and merge with the Tree of Life until the two Trees are One once again.

The Earth and all its inhabitants can live in the perfect co-creative harmony of Oneness—with each other and fully united with Full Source.

To end our spiritual and existential exile, we need to heal the brokenness between men and women—between the masculine and the feminine—that is so prevalent in our lives. There must be a dramatic shift from the bilateral design that holds and expresses the polarized masculine and feminine toward a merged wholeness.

In the image of Jungian archetypes, every man holds within himself the *anima,* the universal feminine, and every woman holds within herself the *animus,* the universal male.[2] To best be whole, a man needs to recognize and embrace his feminine, and a woman needs to recognize and embrace her masculine.

If we crave Oneness for our world, we must first find it in ourselves—in our own beings and in our most intimate relationships. With our ever-evolving consciousness, that integration is beginning right now. We are happily witnessing men and women fragilely and delicately manifesting the harmonization of their internal attributes into the public arena of human interaction.

Over the last fifty years or so, movement has begun. Despite the inequalities and the horrors that still exist between men and women, we have begun to make slow progress. [I am embarrassed to have written that sentence, because it is men who still mostly control the progress, and as a man, I am ashamed that all human beings, regard-less of gender or gender identification, are still not living in equality.]

Still, at least in America, no parents have to tell their daughter: girls can't do that, be in that place, get that education, or do that job. Women attend previously all-male universities; women hold jobs and professions that were once exclusively male. Women are CEOs and corporate presidents and are elected to high government positions throughout the country.

Yet the glass ceiling still exists. There is still stark inequality in pay for work. No one asks a male candidate for a position how he will handle his job after his baby is born. In America it is illegal to ask a woman that question, but not-so-subtle inquiries are still made. In many places the male, hierarchical, authoritarian "old boys' clubs" still exist and flourish. And tragically, in many so-called civilized societies across the world, women are still subjugated to the will of their fathers, husbands, or brothers, and are still denied the most basic human and civil rights.

Our "progress" is not enough! It will never be enough until there is no more discrimination, inequality, and divisiveness between men and women in the public arena. Now is the time, long overdue, for the hierarchical, authoritarian ladders that men build to fall away in favor of the networks and webs that women weave. Now is the time for egalitarianism and balance to enter the workplace and the world—and the human psyche.

The good news is: Women and men here on Earth—as it is for the Divine Feminine and the Divine Masculine in the Heavens—have begun the dance of sympathetic vibration. Many women are already embodying the Shechinah Presence, the Shechinah energy, and are liv-ing the vision of what can be. And many men are waking from spiritual slumber and chauvinistic clumsiness to embrace equality and unity.

The happy truth is that we hold the power and the promise to heal the brokenness and bring wholeness to our world. Shechinah and Source *can* come together in Sacred Union. We can make the Tree of

Life and the Tree of the Knowledge of Good and Evil upright and whole once again.

Here is a prayer/meditation for weaving together the Divine Masculine and the Divine Feminine, for braiding the masculine and feminine here on Earth, and for ending the separation and celebrating the Oneness of God and all humankind.

RIGHTING THE TREE
a tale of Then and Now

For the sake of unifying
the Holy One, Blessed is He and the *Shechinah*, Blessed is She

Once it was:

The peace of Paradise was shattered by discord, and the Center-peace Tree twisted and cracked into two. Life—up. Knowledge—upside down. Masculine—erect. Feminine—inverted.

It is a Tree of Life...and Knowledge

And, so:

The upright Tree lost the beauty of His leaves, and the comfort of His shade, and the nourishment of His fruit. His home-place was shrouded in mystery and lost to human eyes. All that was left was His rigid power

to all who hold on passionately.

And, at the same time:

The Tree that was banished to the underworld embodied Her exile, and embraced all who journeyed with Her. She was grace, and dignity, and eternal hope.

Everyone who sustains Her is happy

And, now:

The pain of separation and disconnection has become too great. The twin burdens of loneliness and exile have become too painful. The healing and reconciliation begins:

Her paths are paths of pleasantness

And, so it becomes:

The long-divided Tree braids its brokenness. She and He blend together in harmony and unity. The Garden awakens and enlivens. New branches sprout, and new seedlings take root throughout Creation. The fabric of the renewed-genesis of existence is woven. Oneness spreads throughout the universe. Peace infuses All That Is.

And, it is so.

And all the paths are Peace.

Re-Turn us unto You,
and we will return
Renew our days as at the very, very Beginning.[3]

One Tree.
Radical Love and Awesome Holiness infuse the world.

TEACH YOUR
CHILDREN WELL

Love and the pathway to holiness are nurtured in the sacred relationship between parent and child.

No child emerges from the womb with a natural-born, inherent worldview.

Kindness, compassion, decency, dignity, selflessness, and the ways of love and holiness are taught and learned attitudes and behaviors. Sadly, so are nationalism, racism, misogyny, homophobia, prejudice, discrimination, bigotry, and hatred.

We, the parents—the Earthly stewards of these precious souls—are the ones who take a totally helpless little baby, completely dependent on us for survival, and oversee this child's physical development and social formation. We are the ones who make the choices and convey the lessons—by word and deed, wittingly and unwittingly—that shape a young person's ethics and values, point of view, and priorities.

We are God's holy partners in nourishing, nurturing, forming, and sustaining a cherished human being on this Earth. As the ancient philosopher Philo taught: "What God is to the world, parents are to their children."

> *A young sister and brother were following their father on a hike up a steep and curvy mountain. As the trek became more dangerous, their mother, who was at the back of the procession, called out to her husband, "Be careful. Our children are walking in your footsteps."*

The stark truth: All it takes is a few minutes of passion to become a parent. It takes a lifetime to *be* a parent. And it is not easy being a parent these days.

As soon as they are old enough to comprehend the daily news, our children hear about violence and warfare and untold human suffering in the four corners of the Earth. They learn about rape and murder and all manner of mayhem just around the corner from home. As they grow older, they are tempted by alcohol and drugs; their lives are threatened by sexually transmitted disease. The pressures to succeed at school and at play are fierce; they worry that at any moment their classroom or playground might be riddled with bullets.

They see a culture increasingly marked by selfishness and self-interest, personal pleasure and instant gratification. They see a world that all too often has a hard time discerning between right and wrong.

They are confused and bewildered. And they are afraid.

It is not easy being a child these days.

So our children desperately need wise guidance and clear direction, unequivocal ethical values and boundless love. Our children need us, their parents who gave them life, to teach them how to live.

It is parents who teach our children how to be a man, how to be a woman, how to be a decent human being.

It is parents who teach our children core values—personal responsibility, hard work, strong ethical principles, and high moral character.

It is parents who teach our children goodness and right, kindness and compassion, faith, holiness, and love.

It is parents who guide our children toward the transcendent world of Spirit.

How can we be the best parents we can possibly be? The key to good parenting is conscious parenting:

- being fully aware—making sure that what we do with our children is well-conceived, well-planned, well-executed;
- being mindful—carefully thinking about the choices we make, the words we speak, the actions we take;

- ❧ being loving—respecting our children as human beings, considering their feelings, responding to their needs;
- ❧ being purposeful—being in touch with our children's inner spirit and cognizant of their place in the universe.

Even in the bewilderment and suffering of the Warsaw ghetto, the great Rabbi-educator Kalonymus Kalman Shapira *zt"l* remembered what is important about human life: "An educator [parent] who wishes to uncover the soul of the child ... must penetrate into the midst of his limited consciousness ... until he reaches the hidden soul-spark."

As long ago as the fourteenth century, the German theologian Meister Eckhart taught: "The seed of God is in us. Given an intelligent farmer and an intelligent farmhand, it will thrive and grow up to God whose seed it is, and, accordingly, its fruit will be God-nature. Pear seeds grow into pear trees, nut seeds grow into nut trees, and God-seeds grow into God."

The task of parenting is to be God's intelligent farmhand, God's partner in the work of creation; to thoughtfully and in full-awareness seek the hidden soul-spark in our children; to know it as God-seed; to carefully nurture it in its unfolding being; to lovingly grow our children's hearts and souls.

With gender appropriateness, "Train up a child in the way he should go, and when he is old, he will not depart from it" (Prov. 22:6).

Here are just a few ways that we can best parent our children toward a life of love and holiness:

1. Sing, Read, and Cultivate Culture.

    In the womb and from their first breaths on Earth, we can expose our children to the melodies, harmonies, rhythms, and words of life. We can give them the great music, literature, art, drama, dance, and museums of human civilization. We can help them be culturally literate. We can show them the great value of Earth's beauty and the natural wonders of our universe.

2. Eat with Them.

   We can nourish not only our children's bodies but also their souls with our presence and conversation at mealtime. We can give them our undivided attention. We can listen to them; talk to them; share our history, wisdom, and guidance.

3. Visit.

   We can expand our children's universe by taking them to visit grandparents, aunts, uncles, cousins to know family legend and lore. And we can make play-dates for them to be with friends to learn socialization and grace. We can introduce them to our friends so that they learn respect and good manners.

4. Take Them to School and Monitor Their Homework and Grades.

   We can let the teacher know that we are partners in our children's education, and we can supervise their learning. The old Welsh poet George Herbert left us with this truth: "One parent is more than one hundred schoolmasters."

5. Turn On the Television and Computer/Turn Off the Television and Computer; Provide Cell Phones/Take Away Cell Phones.

   Modern technology puts the world right before our children's eyes and ears. They can see and virtually experience either the greatest of human civilization, or humanity at its most debased. They can be connected for their safety, mind-expansion, and enjoyment—or they can become dependent upon a machine to do their thinking, imagining, and creating. Parents hold the power of technology in the finger that turns the devices on or off. We can use that power wisely.

6. Create a Safe Space.

    In this uncertain and sometimes frightening world, we can make our homes safe and secure havens for our children. We can give them one little corner of the world where there is trust, well-being, and serenity—a place that is comfortable and comforting.

7. We Cannot—

    —Scream or yell at our children.

    It frightens them.

    —Bully them with our strength or power.

    It intimidates them.

    —Physically abuse them.

    It traumatizes them.

    —Sexually abuse them.

    It wounds them.

    —Lie or violate their trust.

    It scares them.

    —Smoke, Drink, or Do Drugs.

    It damages them.

    If we err and somehow emotionally hurt our children, we can first recognize our mistake, admit our failing, ask forgiveness, and let our love overcome. And if necessary, we can get them the outside professional help that they need to heal. We and our children can grow together.

    As the late First Lady of the United States, Barbara Bush—a fine mother and grandmother herself—once said, "You have to love your children unselfishly. That's hard. But it's the only way."

8. Pray, Meditate, or Be Quiet Together.

    In the chaos of the everyday, we can take a few moments with our children to seek a deep connection beyond this Earth-world. In humility, awe, gratitude, and joy we can sense the wonder of being alive and the Oneness of everything and everyone. We and our children can touch the absolute core of our beings, meet ourselves in ourselves, and shape the unlimited possibility and unbounded potential that is in us.

9. Hug Them, Kiss Them, Tell Them, "I Love You."

    In this uncertain world, our children must be absolutely certain of one thing—that we love them unconditionally with all our hearts and souls. We can assure them over and over again with words and with displays of affection. Love. Love. Love.

10. Teach Them to Swim.

    What a strange ancient injunction for modern parents (BT Kiddushin 29a). But it makes perfect sense. When we teach our children to swim, we teach them how to survive and thrive in a foreign environment. And as parents, we learn how long to hold on and when to let go.

Even as we parents embrace the difficult but profound task of slowly letting go of our children as they grow, we need to remember that as *we* are, so *they* will be. It is told that:

> *A woman brought her son to the great sage Mahatma Gandhi and said, "Please, Master. Please tell my son to stop eating sugar."*
>
> *Gandhi looked deeply into the boy's eyes, and replied, "Madam, please bring your son back to me in two weeks."*
>
> *The woman said, "Please, Master. Please. Cannot you tell him now? Why must we wait for two weeks? And besides, we have come a long way by train. We will have to go home now and come back again. It is a long and expensive trip. Please, Master. Please tell my son right now to stop eating sugar."*
>
> *Again, Gandhi looked deeply into the boy's eyes, and said, "Madam, please bring your son back to me in two weeks."*

The woman had no choice. She and her son returned home, and
two weeks later traveled again to see the Master.

In his holy presence, she once again implored, "Please, Master.
Please tell my son to stop eating sugar."

Gandhi looked deeply into the boy's eyes, and said, "Stop eating
sugar."

"Oh, thank you, Master. Thank you so very much. I am sure
that my son will follow your words and stop eating sugar. But,
please tell me. When we first came to you, why did you send us
away and tell us to come back in two weeks?"

Gandhi looked at the woman and her son and said, "You see,
Madam, it is very simple. Two weeks ago, I was eating sugar."

The children who are being born right now are coming into being in
order to transform our Earth.[1] They are extremely intelligent, highly
gifted, exceptionally talented, deeply intuitive, incredibly creative,
full of energy, self-reliant and self-sufficient, and happily precocious.
They are wise "old souls" who have a keen sense of purpose and destiny. They have come here to shift the paradigms of the old structures,
rules, and authorities in order to build a new world of compassion,
holiness, and love.

For some, the wild imperfection of this world sears their souls, and
in their emotional and spiritual pain they *act out*, don't *go along*, and
don't *get along*. Sometimes they are in high stress and *play out* their
pain through aggressive behavior.

Yet they are not to be judged negatively, treated harshly, diagnosed
flippantly, or medicated blithely. For, in reality these magnificent children carrying their vison of perfection for our world are our pathfind-
ers who react painfully when they see a world that is far less than they
know it must be.

Our precious children are pure channels of God who know and
remember the Divine blueprint for the universe. They are at a higher
soul, or "vibrational" level, than any human beings who have ever
before come to Earth.

This is why being a parent these days is more important than ever. We are the ones who must make sure that our children's holy light is not stifled or extinguished. We are the ones who will encourage and support them as they envision and enact the evolution and transformation of our Earth.

Our children need us.

Our children are counting on us.

We can teach our children well.

We can be their champion.

We can be their hero.

One day, I chanced to meet two small children, a young
girl and her little brother, who were crying.
A short conversation with the children revealed that they were lost.
To the best of my ability, I tried to show them the way.
Whereupon they went down the road singing.

THE RABBI AND
THE PRIEST

The holiness of understanding, acceptance, and love is best built in personal relationships and evolving friendships.

I grew up on the old Southeast Side of Chicago, a neighborhood that, much like other newly middle-class neighborhoods across the country, tried very hard to be a melting pot and mixing bowl for the American dream.

In the late-1940s and early-1950s, when I was young, all the kids played together in the parks and on the playgrounds. We were all good friends.

Then, for kindergarten, some went to the local public school, and some went to Saint Mary Magdalene's, the local parish Catholic school.

By the time I was eight or nine years old, I was being beaten up on a fairly regular basis by my old friends who had learned from their priests and nuns that I, Wayne Dosick, had personally killed their Lord Jesus.

They acted, of course I now know, from the deep-seated prejudice that is born out of ignorance and fear. But the physical blows I received did not hurt nearly as much as the pain of bewilderment and rejection.

The prejudice and fear of the time was not confined to pre-adolescent parochial school boys alone. Sad to say, many of the Jewish grandparents of our generation—grandparents who in their own youth had fled from the Russian Czar and the oppressive governments of Eastern Europe—would spit three times on the sidewalk if forced to walk in front of a church. Long-held hatreds and blind intolerance were part of the sorry lessons of our childhood too.

Then, the winds of sweet change began with a twinkle-eyed pope.

When I was in high school—a building that looked like a five-story, red-brick prison—during one of those four-minute breaks between class periods when we had to go from the first-floor gym to the fifth-floor study hall, a girl ran up to me in the hallway. "Wayne, Wayne," she said, "I forgive you. I forgive you."

Now, there were many girls in that school who might have had reason to forgive me, but she was not one of them. "What is it, Bonnie?" I asked. "For what are you forgiving me?"

"I forgive you for killing Christ," she said.

"What are you talking about? I didn't kill anybody. That was two thousand years ago. I didn't even know him. I wasn't even there."

"It doesn't matter," she said. "I just heard on my transistor radio [remember those?] that the Pope said that we could forgive the Jews for killing Christ."

That, of course was Pope John XXIII, and that was in the midst of Vatican II. Even though young Bonnie did not have the terminology quite right, that Vatican Council signaled a remarkable moment in the two-thousand-year history of Jewish-Christian relations. No longer would the Jews be yoked with the charge of deicide. Two religions—the founding mother and the precious offspring—could begin to regard each other with newfound tolerance, respect, and honor.

And so, in the years since Vatican II, Christians and Jews have begun to learn about each other's faiths and faith communities. We have learned to rejoice in our similarities and respect our differences. We have begun to share in each other's celebrations and participate in each other's ceremonies.

And during this time, with our newfound sensitivity we have opened our arms wide to envelop and embrace our brothers and sisters of other religious faiths and communities—Muslims, whose beginnings are so rooted in the Judaic-Christian experience—and the eastern religions: Buddhism, Hinduism, and more. And we have developed a new and deep appreciation of Native American teachings and traditions. The whole world of the spirit is opening; new light is infusing every corner of our existence.

We have learned that we are all on the same journey, and that our destination is exactly the same. From God, to God. That is the Earthly sojourn; that is our shared calling.

"Wonder of wonders! Miracle of miracles!" Well more than forty years removed from the old neighborhood and the old prejudices, I spent seventeen years as a rabbi on the faculty of a Catholic university—the University of San Diego, a diocesan private liberal arts school—teaching the courses in Jewish Studies in the Department of Religious and Theological Studies. We have come a long way.

The great privilege and blessing of teaching at the University of San Diego was not only that I got to convey Judaism's wisdom to the students at this Catholic university, but that I have come to know and respect the members of the faculty—both priests and lay people—who are fine scholars and pedagogues and who embody a deep personal commitment to Christian teachings, traditions, and values. And they have come to know me and honor both the ancient and the contemporary teachings of the mother-faith.

I was invited to preach from the pulpit of the Immaculata, standing next to a statue of Jesus. Yes, we have come a long way. All of us.

Over the years, I have become very friendly with Father James J. O'Leary, S. J.—fondly known as JJ. He is now one of my closest friends.

JJ is a kind, gentle, deeply spiritual man. He is revered and adored by everyone, for he is the sage and mentor, and kind and compassionate friend to whom many turn for guidance and direction. I have often described him as "a priest who creates holy ground wherever he walks." And—making him even more beloved—he has a warm Irish sense of humor and a great love for the game of golf.

JJ did not know any Jews when he was growing up, and as a youngster he was taught to pray for the "perfidious Jews" because they had killed Christ and didn't accept Jesus as their Messiah.

And I am the one who was beaten up by the Catholic kids in the old neighborhood for killing JJ's Lord.

Yet, we have grown beyond our childhood upbringings to know and appreciate each other's faiths and communities. We have become such close friends and spiritual brothers that I read the Hebrew Scripture at Fr. O'Leary's mother's memorial mass, and he read Psalms at my father's funeral.

Before he moved back to his Province in Milwaukee, JJ and I often had lunch together. We would talk of things that friends discuss—our work, families, backgrounds, training, jobs, university politics, theology, sports. We told each other all those old priest and rabbi jokes. We wondered whether the next Israeli government would bring peace and whether the next Pope would be any more liberal. (He is! And, just like JJ, he's a Jesuit.)

We teased each other. He asked me, "When are you going to eat a ham sandwich?" I replied, "At your wedding reception."

I told him that if the next pope is chosen the way popes should be chosen—by the Holy Spirit—then he would be sure to be the next pope—Pope JJ the First. And, through his amused embarrassment, he told me that if that ever happened, he'd bring me to the Vatican as his closest advisor and give me one of those red *yarmulkes* that the Cardinals wear.

On campus, we were known as the "Stodgy Radicals" because we both cherish the traditions of our faiths—while at the same time we are innovative thinkers who advocate fundamental and sweeping reform and change in the theology, practices, and institutions of our religions.

One of the very best moments for both of us was when a student came up to us and said, "You know, when I came to this university I did not know any Jews. There weren't any where I grew up. And to tell you the truth, I held some prejudice against Jews from all the stories I had heard. But if the two of you can be friends, then I guess that I can meet some Jews and become friendly with them. *You two are a living sermon.*"

Fr. O'Leary and I know that there are certainly theological issues that divide us. But we know that there is much more that unites us as children of God, children of the universe.

And now, any time Catholicism is harshly criticized or under attack, Fr. JJ knows that I will stand up for his faith. And I know that any time Judaism—the Jewish religion, people, or state—is criticized, Fr. JJ will stand up with me for my faith.

We cannot be enemies because we are such good friends.

And, if a priest and a rabbi can grasp hands in friendship—then imams, gurus, roshis, Tribal Elders, shamans, and spiritual leaders of the eastern religions can too.

And every Christian, Jew, Muslim, Buddhist, Hindu, Native American—and person of every faith, creed, race, and color can too.

How?

We can begin.

We can meet a person of another faith. Have coffee. Have lunch. Take a walk. Sit on a park bench. Watch your children play. Talk. Listen. Ask. Understand. Accept. Embrace. Make a friend. Lose an enemy.

We can ask our friend to be a moderating influence on the more fiery, the more radical elements in his or her faith community—to help soften the demeanor, the rhetoric, and the conduct of those whose ethnic, theological, political, or cultural passions lead to acrimony rather than harmony.

We can ask our friend to help create a world where the common cause of all humanity triumphs and endures, where old hurts are healed by newfound love, where all God's children touch hearts and hands in peace.

Long-felt pain can turn to vibrant healing.

Long-term intolerance can turn into sweet harmony.

A new age of love and holiness is coming.

And we are here.

RE-FRAMING

"The universe is full of magical things patiently waiting for our senses to grow sharper."[1]

Sometimes, we see, but we do not see. We hear, but we do not hear. We think we know—but do we?

When we raise our awareness and our consciousness, we can grasp what is right before us in new and revealing ways.

How?

Re-Frame.

We can Re-Frame the ordinary and the everyday into a spiritual practice. Usually, it takes no change in how we act. It is only a change in how we perceive and think about what we see and do. And it takes just a brief moment.

Here are a few possibilities. As we experience these and feel their impact on our lives, we may discover many others that speak to us.

1.   Take Out the Garbage.

The Bible tells us that before he dressed in his fancy ceremonial garb and conducted the now long-gone sacrificial rituals, the High Priest would put on a simple linen garment (the sweat suit of his day) and take the cold ashes from the previous evening's sacrifice out to the garbage dump (Lev. 6:3–4).

Like the priest of old, when we take out the garbage we surrender to the realities of life—no matter how awkward or heavy or smelly they are. All pretense falls away; we are humbled. No matter how high our status in the outside world, we know that on the inside we are just like every other human being on Earth. And metaphorically, we can also throw away the *schmutz*—the soiled, broken, unhappy parts of our lives.

We can reframe taking out the garbage and feel the satisfaction of a job well-done and a purpose well-fulfilled.

2. Light a Candle.

Many religious and faith communities use candles for ceremony and ritual; some use candlelight to facilitate meditation. Many people use candles to set a mood or an atmosphere for dinner parties or for romance.

We can Re-Frame the candle. What was the very first act of creation? "God said, 'Let there be light.'" And we are taught to remember the moment of creation, for every soul is connected to that very beginning.

When we light a candle, we who are created in the image of God, imitate God. We bring light to the darkness; we center ourselves in a new beginning.

If we take a long enough time—or it may take only a few seconds—to stare into the candle flame, we may be able to get in touch with that primordial moment of creation. And if we can do that, then very possibly we can get in touch with the Primordial Creator, God.

We can see not just a candle, not just a flame. We can see God.

3. Be in Amazement, Awe, and Perpetual Gratitude.

On a walk, our child (grandchild, student, young friend) might say, "Mom, (Dad, Grandma, Grandpa), look at that tree. It's so big, and its leaves are so green and pretty."

We could reply, "Yes, it is. And I remember from

my study of trees when I was just a little older than you, that the deeply ridged bark and oval shape of the leaves with the points on the end means that it is an elm tree."

Ah. A fine lesson in dendrology.

Or we can Re-Frame our response and say, "Yes. And what a great gift God has given us. The tree is so grand, so regal, so magnificent, so awesome. It is a wonder of nature. Its bark is so strong, and its leaves give us such deep shade, and its buds feed the little animals. Thank You, God, for giving us such a beautiful, majestic blessing for all our senses to take in and enjoy.

Ah. What a lesson in infinite gratitude.

4. Exercise.

We know that exercise—vigorous physical activity in its many varieties—is good for our bodies. It helps keep us healthy and well.

We can Re-Frame exercise to be not just for our bodies, but also for our souls. Our souls—the animation of our lives and the consciousness and conscience of our beings—need and deserve our mindful attention. We can disengage from the onslaught of life. We can unplug from the electronic devices that seem to run our lives. We can: think, contemplate, pray, meditate, read, sing, dance, dig deep into our beings. We can set our intention to be fully present to the Divine Presence who continually gives us breath and life and asks us to be the fullest, most loving, most holy human we can be.

We can be soulful and soul-filled.

5. Smile. Say, "Hello."

So many people, Americans in particular, seem to

live in a cocoon. We walk down the street and never make eye contact with another. We stand in checkout lines at the grocery store and do not speak to the people in front of or behind us. We sit in doctors' waiting rooms in complete silence.

The power of a smile, the simplest greeting, has power beyond imagination. Our smile will often be met with a smile. Our "Hello" will often be met with a response. Connecting to one person at a time in a simple gesture of recognition means that instead of being separate entities occupying our own little spaces we begin to weave together a network of humanity.

These days it might be a little scary to offer a smile or talk to a total stranger. But if we can Re-Frame how we greet our fellow human beings, we can begin to reframe the entire fabric on which our world is built.

6.　Go into The Void.

"The Void" sounds as if it is a scary place of dark, empty, nothingness. Why would anyone want to go there?

We can Re-Frame the idea of The Void to know that it is the place of the finest creation. The world was created when the first Light came from out of the darkness. Trees, flowers, and vegetation grow from seeds planted in the deep darkness of the soil. Babies form, are nurtured, and grow into becoming in the darkness of a mother's womb.

When we go to dark places, we do not have to be afraid. We can be joyful. For from there, we will find and shape our most wondrous ideas; our greatest creativity; our finest essence; our deepest, most ardent love.

Ultimately, nothing—no-thing—is Void, for God is

everywhere. And everywhere we go, even to the deepest depths of the dark and unknown, there is God.

7.   Have *Holy Chutzpah*.

Chutzpah is the Yiddish word for unmitigated gall;
unflinching, intrepid boldness; fearless nerve.

We have not come into this life to simply (as
Shakespeare would have it) "strut and fret our hour
upon the stage," to fritter away our lives, and then to
"be heard no more." And surely, we have not come into
being to hate or destroy.

We can Re-Frame any notion of a vapid, empty life
that has little direction or purpose.

We are here to use our inherent wisdom, acquired
knowledge, talents, and skills to move the world forward; to build a better world; to embody the vision of
a world of goodness, harmony, tranquility, and peace.
We have come into being to praise, to labor, and to
love.

Sometimes it takes real *chutzpah* to advocate for the
right, speak up for change, shake up the status quo,
tilt windmills, lead into the as yet unknown, announce
discovery, advance the world beyond its current com-
forts, face opposition and adversity with grace and
determination. Sometimes we need to shake our fists
at the world, be the mad prophet who says, "I'm not
going to take this anymore."

We can have *holy chutzpah*. We can know that we
are the hearts and hands of God, bringing Radical
Loving and Awesome Holiness to our world.

8.   Be Conscious of Every Moment.

We go about our lives from hour to hour, day to
day, year to year. There are times of celebration and

times of sorrow, peak experiences and the ordinary,
and every day.

We can Re-Frame and be conscious. In every single moment is the whole of creation; the past and
the future all converge in the now—this single, solitary millisecond in time. There are 86,400 seconds
in every day. We cannot waste one of them. "There is
a time to every purpose under Heaven" (Eccles. 3:1).
Life's greatness, capriciousness, vicissitudes, changes,
choices, decisions, direction—all happen in one
moment. Life and death are held in a nanosecond.
From out of one unique moment, nothing is ever the
same again.

We cannot take any precious moment for granted.
We can embrace time and shape it the best way that
we can. And we can always be ready for whatever may
come, for everything new under the sun is waiting in
the very next second. Re-Framing is all a matter of
perspective, of how we choose to see the world.

A man got on a bus and found himself sitting
next to a a young woman who was wearing only one shoe.
"I see that you have lost a shoe," he said.
"No sir," she replied. "I found one."

CREATING SACRED COMMUNITY

Beyond personal and family relationships is the vision of building a world of love and holiness, awe, gratitude, and joy by creating a conscious, sacred worldwide community.

It is no easy task because there is great diversity; widely differing beliefs, values, and practices; competing agendas; and self-interest, self-aggrandizement, and rigid stubbornness.

Yet "how good and pleasant it is for brothers [and sisters] to dwell together in unity and harmony" (Ps. 133:1).

What is right on the micro levels, in our own neighborhoods and towns, easily translates into the macro—what is right for our countries and our world.

How do we create communities that are connected and cohesive, where people feel invested, heeded, respected, and honored? How do we build and nurture the world of love and holiness that we so desperately need and crave? Ancient wisdom can teach us and show us the way:

1. At the absolute center of creating a sacred community, we place God. Without God, our endeavors are ultimately hollow and empty. With God's guidance, we have a clear direction. We—all of us—are Your people, and You are our God.

2. We cannot forget. We cannot stray. We keep God and God's Divine Design right in front of us.

3. We do not exist in a vacuum or off the time continuum. We are guided by the triumphs and the tragedies, the acts and

decisions (including the successes and mistakes) of those who have come before us, and who struggled with many of the same issues we face. There is great wisdom in the knowledge and experience of our Elders, who are our sages. We honor them and listen to them. They have much to tell.

4. Everyone—people of all ages, genders, races, ethnicities, religions, and abilities—is included in our community. No one is to be shunned or excluded, but welcomed and fully integrated.

5. Sometimes, for a wide variety of reasons people choose to absent themselves from the community. Yet they are an integral part of the whole and cannot be ignored or forgotten. We reach out to them. Our doors are always open to them.

How do we give ultimate purpose to our conscious, sacred community?

1. All that we do is for the purpose of bringing love and holiness into our world.

2. Each one of us is a unique human being with a special task. We raise our words and our deeds to the highest level of service to God.

3. Our job is to end the brokenness and to lift up every inhabitant of our Earth to a life of decency and dignity.

4. We do not judge people by outward appearance. All people—regardless of race, gender, sexual preference, ability or disability, belief or nonbelief—are equal in God's eyes and should be in ours. Everyone is a valuable member of the community, and the only thing that counts is on the inside—the content of character.

5. We can visit the ill, care for the elderly, attend to the dead, comfort the mourner, care for the widow and the orphan, protect the environment, care for animals. A community is only as strong as its most vulnerable member. Any and every child of God who is in need, needs us to be God's heart and hands here on Earth.

6. We have surely earned the material resources we have, yet all that we have is a gift and a blessing from God. We can share our financial resources to help sustain the community and its sacred work.

7. There is great power in words. Words can celebrate and elevate the human spirit or cut like the sharpest sword and crush the human spirit. Words can weave together communities or tear them apart. Every word that comes from our mouths can be good, sweet, and holy.

8. No matter what the issue, no matter what the conflict, no matter how our personal feelings are celebrated or diminished, it is always worth the effort, and sometimes the pain, to stay in the arena, to keep open the discussion and the pathway to resolution. There is always hope; there is always possibility. We never give up. We always do our very best. We always remember that we are building for those who come after us.

9. We can let our every word and deed be for love and peace: love and peace in our home, love and peace in our community, love and peace in our country, love and peace in the world—the celebration of all humankind embraced in love and peace.

In sacred community there is history, energy, responsibility, power, friendship, unity, and destiny. In sacred community, there is holiness and love of connection.

> *A sociologist reported that the elderly men of a California beach town who got up every morning to go to a worship service lived longer than their contemporaries who did not go to the service.*
>
> *Did their prayers to God make them healthier, grant them longer life?*
>
> *Yes. And more likely, the ones who got up and went to worship knew that there were others there waiting for them to be part of the communal service. They could not stay in bed because others*

were counting on them. They felt a sense of purpose and mission, an obligation to their friends that was more important than their personal choices. They felt that they were an integral part of a group. They felt important and needed. That is what kept them alive.[1]

The selfless Mother Teresa left us an inspiring mandate: "The greatest good is what we can do for one another .... I alone cannot change the world, but I can cast a stone across the waters to create many ripples."

American President Bill Clinton took the Mother's words to heart and gave us our reality and our shared mission: "For good or ill, we live in an interdependent world. We can't escape each other. Therefore, we have to spend our lives building a global community of shared responsibilities, shared values, shared benefits."[2]

We can encircle each other.

We can connect with each other.

We can inspirit each other.

We can commit to each other.

We can make a world of holiness.

We can make a world of love.

We can make a world of peace.

Because at our core, our souls know who we are.

And ...

We can become as big as our souls.
We can rise up.
Take the leap.
And God will catch us.

THE POWER OF ONE

We praise our ancestors, our teachers, our friends, our colleagues, the members of our community for their gifts of Love and Holiness.

Now we ask—how do we become good ancestors to our descendants? What legacy will we leave to our children and to generations of our lineage yet unborn?

How do we each take our place in the ongoing process of the universe?

We give the work of our hearts and our hands to repair, to heal, the brokenness of the world in order to bring it closer and closer to perfection—the ultimate vison and promise of a world of harmony and peace. The measure of our days, the way we have made our contribution to a just and peaceful world, will be determined by how well we manifest love and holiness through service to others.

We begin at home. We serve our family.

Remember the vows you made—to your wife, your husband, your partner—when you committed your lives to each other. Remember the unspoken vows you made to your children when you brought them into this world.

You can make your home a sanctuary, a safe and secure shelter and haven from the hectic, noisy, and often tempestuous chaos of the outside world. Your home can be a place of Radical Loving and Awesomely Holy gathering for your family, your friends, and spiritual seekers who come into your space. Your home can be a place where the love of God is always present, and the word of God is a guide and an inspiration.

A caution: All too often these days, "High Tech" seems to be

overtaking "High Touch."¹ And sometimes the art of conversation—
even the act of communication—between spouses, partners, and children is getting lost.

> *Not long ago, my wife and I were in a restaurant. At a nearby
> table there was a family of five—mother and father, a boy I
> would guess to be about fifteen, and two young girls, maybe eight
> and five.*
>
> *Each person was staring down at a cell phone—yes, even the
> five-year old. All of them were busy reading and tapping at the
> keyboards. Except to place their food orders with the server, we
> did not hear any of them utter one word. They did not speak
> with each other during the entire meal, until the father asked,
> "Everyone finished?" They all nodded and got up to leave.*

How sad. Technology and the growing power of "Artificial
Intelligence" is a great blessing and surely has its most helpful place
in this ever-more-complex world. But we cannot let it replace the
incredible value of human contact, human interaction.

Then take your love and your holiness into your community, into
your country, into the world.

We can bring meaning into our lives, we can bring Love and
Holiness into our world when we move out of self-isolation, out of
our homes and our own individual concerns, and begin to talk with
each other, listen to each other, communicate with each other from a
deep, sincere, and sensitive place.

> *When I was very young, our neighborhood gas station was
> owned by a jovial fellow named Wally.*
>
> *When my father pulled our car into the station, Wally would
> quickly come out from his little office and begin to fill the tank. He
> checked the oil, checked the pressure in the tires, cleaned the wind-
> shield wipers, and washed all the car windows—all the while
> chattering about the weather, the White Sox and the Cubs, city*

politics. And he was the best source of neighborhood news and gossip. When he had completed all his tasks, Wally would say, "That does it for today. All set. Thank you for your business, Mr. Dosick. See you next time." My father would pay the amount on the pump, and just before we drove off, as if he were keeping a little secret from my father, Wally would hand a little toy or a lollipop to my sister and me. All for twenty-four cents a gallon.

If there were anything wrong with the car, my father would take it into Wally's service bay. Or if the car would not start on a cold morning, he would call Wally at the station to come tow the car, and Wally would swiftly fix the problem with great mechanical skill and cheerful service at a fair and reasonable price. Our family trusted Wally.

Today, I buy most of my gasoline at a station in my neighborhood. I probably spend well more than a thousand dollars a year at that place. I pump my own gas, wash my own windows, check my own oil. No one comes to help me. And no one even takes my money. I put my credit card into a little slot in the gas pump, and somewhere in cyberspace, the financial transaction is completed.

No one at that station knows me. No one ever thanks me for my business. I've tried going into the little store at the station where they sell soft drinks, candy, and lottery tickets. But even when I buy a bottle of water or an ice cream cone, the clerk hardly looks up at me, or says hello.

I am a customer without name or identity, nothing more to that business owner than another consumer adding to the bottom-line profits.

If we do not even know each other, how can we relate to each other? How can we see each other as human beings? How can we see the Face of God in each other's faces?

That is why we crave human connection. We need each other. So in your family and in the greater human family—talk, talk, talk. And listen, listen, listen.

Sometimes it seems as if the needs are so great, the world's problems and pain so overwhelming, that we are paralyzed into inaction. As the plaque on President John F. Kennedy's desk told: "The sea is so great, and my boat is so small." What to do? Where to begin? How to help?

Our guiding principle is simple: "Let all you do be done with love" (1 Cor. 16:14).

In our love for other human beings, we can hear their voices and their cries, and see their need and their desperation.

We are in awe of the "first responders" who rush into burning houses, collapsing buildings, raging rivers, and mass shootings at the risk of their own lives to try to save the lives of total strangers. They are completely selfless. They merit and deserve our incredible admiration and unending gratitude.

Yet, of course, with some notable exemplary heroic exceptions this is rarely the path for all but the most highly trained, the most dedicated, the most courageous. Still, these humble and self-effacing public servants set a standard for all of us.

So when disaster or tragedy strikes, we who are not on the front lines, become the home-front supporters. We reach out to our fellow human beings in trouble and need, affirming our place as part of the human family. We wrap them in our concern, our compassion, our love. We collect and distribute food, water, and clothing; we give money and time.

Sadly, all too often, in time our embrace of all humanity begins to fade. So we ask, how can we sustain our feelings and actions long beyond the moment of crisis? By serving the continual mandate and mantra: Do good. Do better. Do the best. And then, do some more.

This is a lesson, too, for business, industry, and multinational corporations. To be sure, there is a need for profit and increasing shareholder value. Yet the highest calling is to serve consumers and community with the finest product or service, and to be the exemplar of communal citizenship through leadership, responsibility, and generosity. In business, it is not only the art of the deal, but the art of human connection.

And our service is the work not only in moments of disaster, but also in response to the tremendous needs and yearnings of the every-day. Whatever, wherever, for whomever, there is need—go. You can respond with your love.

> *One day, a man fell down in the snow. He called out, "Help me! Please help me."*
> *A monk came and lay down beside him in the snow.*
> *The man got up and went away.*

F.A.N.A.M.I.: "Find A Need And Meet It."

We can give our talents, our skills, our work, our commitment to myriad places and people who need help. We can serve. Volunteer. Donate. Advocate. Enable. Support. Encourage.

Our service to each other need not be time-consuming or arduous. But it can be a powerful blessing to those we help. To a person who needs a pair of pants, we can give a pair of pants. And if he needs a pair of pants, he probably needs a pair of socks too. So, we can give a pair of socks.

We can visit an ill friend and bring a meal, or a pot of soup, or a chocolate chip cookie. And if our friend has been ill for a while, maybe the bed needs changing or the floor needs washing. So, we can change the bed or wash the floor.

During the local blood drive, we can give a pint of blood. The physical characteristics or skin color of the recipient does not matter. Everyone's blood is red.

We can be mentors to students who need help with their studies, or who need a role model, or just a pal, in their lives. A few hours of our time can mean the difference between failure or success, self-doubt or self-esteem, a bleak or a bright week—or future—for a young person in our community.

An example of what really happened: It is said of an ancient sage that when he went to the marketplace, if he needed only one portion of meat, he would buy two; if he needed only one bunch of vegetables, he would buy two—one for himself and one for the hungry in his town.[2]

When my son was young, we tried to put this custom into modern day practice.

Every time we went to the supermarket, we would buy one extra item of nonperishable food—a box of cereal, a can of tuna fish, a package of macaroni and cheese, a jar of peanut butter.

We put the food directly into a brown paper bag that we kept in the trunk of the car, and when the bag was full, we would take it to one of the local food pantries or soup kitchens.

It was really a very simple way of giving to the hungry folks in our community; it took little time or effort and it cost only a few dollars a week.

One day in the market, I took a box of Cheerios from the shelf and said to my son, "How about these Cheerios for our food gift this week?"

Seth, who was about five or six years old at the time, grabbed the box out of my hand and said, "No!"

I watched him put the Cheerios back on the shelf and, rather amazed, I asked, "Why not? Why shouldn't the Cheerios be our food gift for today?"

With righteous indignation, Seth reached up as far as he could and took a different box of cereal from the shelf, held it up to show me, and said, "Today we are getting Sugar Frosted Flakes, because there are hungry kids out there too, and kids like Sugar Frosted Flakes better than they like Cheerios."

In that instant, my young son taught me to see not a category of people—the "hungry," the "needing," "the poor"—but the faces of the people we were helping. And, as we already know, if we can truly see the face of another, then we can see the Face of God.

We can reach out with the passions and the intensity of our being. We can reach out in Radical Loving. We can reach out in Awesome Holiness, knowing that the promptings of our heart and the work of our hands elevate the human spirit.

If anyone has the world's goods and sees his
brother in need, yet closes his heart against him,
how does God's love abide in him?
Little children, let us not love in word or talk,
but in deed and in truth. (1 John 3:17–18)

We can serve in Radical Loving and Awesome Holiness.

When we reveal our faces to each other—when we see the Face of God reflected in the face of another—then world redemption can come.

"One person can make a difference and every person should try."[3]

"We must live as if the fate of all the world totally depends on a single moment."[4]

It does.

THE POWER OF ALL

It used to be that America was a "front porch" country. We knew our neighbors and had block parties on the Fourth of July. Even though there were still plenty of gritty inner-city neighborhoods, and poverty and crime, and a scary Cold War necessitating the "under the desk" air-raid drills at school, 1950s television programs like *Ozzie and Harriet* and *Leave It to Beaver* painted a totally different picture. Newly built suburban homes had a station wagon in the driveway, a basketball hoop over the garage, a recreation room in the basement, and a loyal dog lounging on the perfectly manicured front lawn. These were idyllic places where all problems could be solved in thirty minutes, with ample time out for commercials.

But the 1960s brought upheaval and massive change.

No longer would the presumed authority of parents, teachers, clergy, and government go unchallenged. No longer would the past be the unquestioned blueprint for the future.

The streets were filled with massive civil rights demonstrations and equally massive antiwar rallies. Two presidents were toppled by passionate public sentiment. Musical, sexual, feminist, and drug culture revolutions changed the face of America forever. America became a country where everybody was encouraged to "do your own thing."

Because I am such a baseball fan, it pains me to say this, but the move to individualism was fueled by—of all things—*the great American pastime*, when in 1972 the Supreme Court of the United States mandated free agency for baseball players.

Until then, each Major League baseball team owned the services of its players, and the players were totally dependent on and at the mercy of the team for contracts, salaries, and working conditions.

While this constituted almost indentured servitude of the players to the teams, it had one benefit. The players were part of a team that was representative of its city. There was great fan-loyalty to the team, and, in turn, the players became part of the community.

While free agency is rightly celebrated as affirming the civil and labor rights of every individual worker and hailed as a great victory for the strength of labor unions that helped build America, baseball—and America—were forever changed.

Now, players change teams as often as they change socks. Rather than their priority being the good of the team, or the pride of a city, with a few notable exceptions, they care mostly about their own personal achievements and statistics that will make them most appealing, and will earn them more compensation from the highest bidding team.

That attitude has made its way into much of American society. Instead of being a soft, embracing blanket that envelops us all, much of America has become a frayed patchwork quilt of special interests.

For so many, the prevalent theme has become *me*. Me. Me. Me.

My needs. *My* desires. *My* values. *My* choices. *My* demands.

We have become a nation that is defined not by its greater whole, but by its wildest extremes—black and white and brown, men and women, straight and gay, rich and poor, the powerful and the powerless. Person against person. Group against group. Cause against cause. We have become a nation that can hardly pass a bill in Congress anymore without compromising principle to political expediency.

We have few agreed-upon common values, little clear direction. We are constantly in fear of being swamped by the wave of narrow self-interest and the militant self-protection of "Me-ism."

What has happened to the common good? The greater good? The greatest good? What has happened to America—one nation indivisible?

What happens when we think and act only for ourselves, and do not respond to and even ignore our brothers and sisters, especially in their times of greatest need?

And we are, at the very same time, a nation beset by the plague of "Not Me-ism." Time and time again, we see people unwilling to take responsibility for their actions, unwilling to accept the consequences of their conduct, blaming others for their plight. Not Me. Not Me.

I'm not guilty. It's not my fault. I did it because (choose one or many): I was underprivileged. I was over-indulged. I was discriminated against because of my color, race, ethnic background, religion, gender, sexual preference, age. I was abused as a child. I was battered as an adult. I trusted someone else. I was never able to trust anyone. I was betrayed, duped—used by father, mother, child, spouse, partner, doctor, lawyer, accountant, therapist, priest, minister, rabbi, imam, the police, the government. Not me! I'm not responsible. I'm not the perpetrator. I'm the victim.

In all too many instances these cries are sadly correct. Yet, in all too many instances they are excuses, rationalizations, weak justifications.

Our community is our Noah's Ark. Without fail, it can and must always have room—and compassion—for everyone.

There is no place in a decent society for selfishness and self-centeredness. And there is no place for shunning responsibility, blaming others, dismissing obligation.

There is, instead, an urgent, critical need for communal obligation, shared responsibility, self-sacrifice, and the common good. We succeed best at being human and humane when we feel part of a family, a community, a group, a clan, a tribe. We share wisdom, learning, experience, energy, strength. We are better for being with each other.

The only way that America and many other countries around the globe will prosper and succeed—indeed, in some cases continue to exist in any constructive and meaningful way—is to restore the torn fabric of our society, to reaffirm the sense of the communal good through communal participation and responsibility.

It will not be easy to shift a mindset that has been growing and festering for decades. It will not even be easy to redefine the common good. But it is an effort worth every bit of energy that people and governments can devote. For, either we band together to forge a new strength in numbers, or we continue to devolve into individual fragments that will eventually break apart and break us.

An old tale:

> *The inhabitants of a small town in a faraway place were eagerly awaiting the arrival of the mystic Sage.*
>
> *There was great need for the wisdom that the Sage would give them because there was great tension and fragmentation and bitterness in the community.*
>
> *This was going to be a rare opportunity to air their differences and their conflicts and receive guidance and direction, so they spent a great deal of time preparing the questions to ask the holy One.*
>
> *When the great Sage finally arrived, she could immediately sense the tension and stress in the community.*
>
> *The Sage said nothing; she just gazed into the eyes of all the people and then began to hum a haunting melody. Slowly, slowly, everyone began to join in the humming. She started to sing, and they sang along with her. She swayed and began to dance. Soon the people rose from their seats and danced with her. It was not long before they were all so absorbed in the chant and the dance that they were lost to everything else on Earth.*
>
> *Every person was so caught up in the communal energy that the tension was eased; every person was healed from the inner fragmentation that was keeping them from loving each other.*
>
> *It was an hour—or maybe much more time—before the dance slowed down. With their stress drained out of them, they sat in deep, meditative silence. Feelings of calm, and acceptance, and amiability, and newfound happiness began to fill the room.*

The Sage then spoke her only words of the evening: "I trust that I have answered all your questions."

The whole can again become stronger than the sum of its singular parts. Together. All of us. Together!

When the task seems too great for any one of us—even for all of us together—we can ask God to be present in our lives to give us help and protection, good counsel and wise guidance, wisdom and insight, hope and strength, comfort and support. We can ask God to help us embody and reflect the Divine through a life of goodness and kindness, caring and sharing, justice and compassion, Radical Loving and Awesome Holiness.

Oh, God,
Open our eyes
that we may see You
in our brothers and sisters.
Open our hearts
that we may love each other
as You love us.
Renew us in Your spirit,
and make us One.
—(adapted) Mother Teresa

Now, it is time for *tachlis*—the Yiddish word for the nitty-gritty, the bottom line, the really real.

There is a didactic tension, a delicate balance, between individual freedoms and the greater good of a society. As the old adage goes, "Your freedom ends where my nose begins."[1]

Still: As controversial and as inflammatory is this may be to some—in America and surely throughout the rest of the world—*get the guns off the streets.*

Period.

Guns kill.

Yes. People pull the trigger. But it is guns that kill.

The litany of horrific mass shootings, crime-related shootings, gang shootings, drive-by shootings, random shootings, and—God help us—police shootings, grows longer every day. The searing grief of the families of the murdered tears at our souls.

Enough.

Enough of being "heartbroken."

Enough of "thoughts and prayers."

Enough of the candlelight vigils, the heart-wrenching memorial services, and the forlorn flowers and teddy bears brought to killing sites.

Enough of vibrant lives being snuffed out by both the calculating and the deranged.

Enough "unspeakable sadness."

It is time to speak out! This is no longer about "gun control," background checks, tweaking registration laws, or banning a certain bullet.

It can no longer be about fiddling around the edges of real reform.

Here and in the great cities of the world—in the nightclubs and restaurants; the markets and malls; the churches, synagogues, and mosques; the subways; the schools; and on the streets—stop guns from killing.

Keep guns out of the hands of the terrorists.

Keep guns out of the hands of the criminals.

Keep guns out of the hands of the mentally ill.

Keep guns out of the hands of the angry, disaffected, and disillusioned.

Keep guns out of the hands of the "lone wolf."

Keep guns out of the hands of the hated-filled, the vengeful, and the violent.

We can debate all we wish about Second Amendment freedoms, gun control laws, and the sport of hunting—but get assault weapons, AK-47s, AR-15s, and other weapons of mass destruction out of the hands of evil-doers.

In New Zealand, when more than fifty people were killed in a recent mass shooting, it took the Government only two weeks to ban citizens from owning AK-15 rifles. In America, where more than one hundred people a day are killed by guns, there is still not the political will or courage to ban these deplorable weapons.

Perhaps it is even time to revisit the United Sates Supreme Court decision on the Second Amendment that protects an individual's right to possess a firearm unrelated to service in a militia.[2] Surely it is time to reevaluate a law from 1791, when life was so fundamentally different than it is now. A gun then is not a gun now. The law of our land has to reflect this reality.

And surely it is time to keep the big money of the pro-gun lobbyists out of the campaign coffers of our elected officials.

It is time for the gun control lobby to out-fundraise, out-publicize, out-lobby, and out-vote, those who allow guns to be in the hands of the criminals, the mentally unstable, the hate-filled terrorist.

We can no longer let financial support influence life and death on our streets. It is time to say to politicians: If you take a penny from the gun lobby, if you vote as the gun lobby advocates, then we will recruit new candidates, raise new money, and we will vote you out of office.

And surely it is time to put monies (that were once there, but were stripped away) back into the federal budget to sufficiently fund and vigorously support the mental hospitals and out-patient treatment centers, the jails and the prisons.

Although it will not be easy, this is not a facile or a futile plea: keep guns out of the hands of killers and potential killers. Stop guns from killing. Now! We cannot "sit idly by the blood of our brothers and sisters" (Lev. 19:16), while people are slaughtered in what are supposed to be our safe cities and byways.

Yes. The rights of individuals must be respected, but they must be balanced and tempered by the common good, the greater good, the greatest good.

More *tachlis*.

When the Internet was invented and established, it was rightly hailed as an instrument of good. It has the potential to break down the hierarchical, authoritarian structure of so many of our traditional systems and to link citizens of the world in open, transparent, egalitarian, and equitable communication.

In so many ways, this is exactly what the Internet has accomplished.

Here is one small example, which I cite because it is in my field, and I am familiar with its impact. It used to be that if one wanted to write a book, he or she would have to: compose the manuscript; get peer review; get endorsements; find an editor; get an agent who would solicit a publisher; have the book accepted by an editorial board whose decision most often depended on many factors beyond the quality of the book; have the manuscript edited again; wait for months (often years) for the book to be published; get a publicist and/ or a marketer; travel or sit for interviews; get invited to bookstores and public appearances to promote the book—and wait for months or even years for a royalty check.

Now, with the Internet all that a writer needs is a few minutes and a computer, and within nanoseconds his/her writing is disseminated all over the world.

In so many ways, this is wonderful because all the intervening layers between the writer and the reader have been eliminated. Yet in so many ways, this new methodology has been disastrous because there is no outside review, perspective, discernment, mindfulness, mediation, balance, or prudence.

So too often, the Internet has sadly and tragically become an instrument for dissemination of hate-filled evil. The so-called "Dark Web" has become a place where repulsive racism, repugnant antigay babble, crude misogyny, vile anti-Semitism and anti-Muslim rants, vulgar white nationalism and white supremacy, blind prejudice, sexual exploitation, and all manner of loathsome abominations have places to seethe and flourish. It is a place where people become radicalized;

where rage is fostered; where civil disobedience, criminality, and violence are celebrated; and where a call to killing is encouraged.

Now, in some twisted way this has a somewhat positive effect on society, because it often brings the haters, bigots, and extremists of our society out from the secretive and dark places where they are hiding and exposes them in the sunlight of a decent, just, good, loving world.

But tragically, the underground network of the Internet—and the subterranean cells of self-righteous, angry, dangerous humanity it fosters—most often still hides more than it exposes.

Hate speech, be it verbal or online, leads to hate crimes, and very often perpetrators of crimes and mass killings have been highly influenced, motivated, radicalized, and emboldened by the Internet.

More. The Internet is used by criminals to scam innocent people and steal their identity, resources, credit, and good names. It is used to hack into legitimate businesses and governments to steal information, alter outcomes, prevent political intent, and—yes—influence elections. Social media sites, in their eagerness for dominance and revenue, often accept advertising filled with untruths and propaganda that unduly distorts and influences.

There is no mediation or easy contradiction of the blatant lies and falsehoods that float around cyberspace, and few ways to counter the distortions. Cybercrime zooms around the world with lightning speed and has the very real potential and power to shatter the lives of individuals, communities, and countries.

First Amendment rights granted by the United States Constitution protect much of this hate-filled rhetoric. Over the centuries, the courts have placed some limits on free speech when the safety, rights, and protections of others are violated. But the original constitutional framers could never have possibly anticipated the challenges that the Internet would bring to a free and open society, where the use of high technology can bring such potential pain and suffering.

It is time for great legal minds to propose ways that the Internet can be an instrument of good and not evil by protecting not only the rights of those who invoke First Amendment freedoms, but also of those whose lives—and deaths—are so profoundly at stake.

More *tachlis*.

Words matter.

Leaders of nations set an atmosphere for their countries through the words of their mouths. Their tone can be peace-loving and uplifting, supportive and encouraging to every citizen. Or their tone can be hate-filled, fear-mongering, and plainly untrue—encouraging divisiveness and pitting their citizens against each other. Or their tone can be indifferent and unresponsive to the needs and the plights of their people.

In contemporary America, recent leadership has turned a deaf ear, a blind eye, and a muted voice to virulent and violent acts against races, women, gays, Jews, and Muslims—and to the plight of the most needing in society.

There are not good people on both sides of evil acts. But lack of condemnation and silence proclaims assent. So perpetrators continue to wreak havoc; their horrific acts are on the rise. This is why the Bible teaches, "The tongue has the power of life and death" (Prov. 18:21). As apocryphal as the legend may be—it was not only in ancient times but, tragically, today too—that "Nero fiddles while Rome burns."

Leaders must know: make your tone positive and inspiring to every one of your citizens. If your tone is not suitable and worthy, if your tone brings anxiety and conflict instead of confidence and trust, then *change your tone*. Or your citizens will go to the ballot box to *change their leader*.

None of this will be easy—neither the changes in attitudes and perceptions, nor the changes that will rid us of the violence born of guns, nor the restraints and the balance on the Internet, nor the recognition and full understating of leaders about how they must lead.

But we can begin.

A woman dreamed that she walked into a new shop in the marketplace and, to her great surprise, she found God behind the counter.

"What do you sell here?" she asked.

"Everything your heart desires," replied God.

"That is wonderful! If that is so, then I want peace of mind, and love, and wisdom, and happiness, and freedom from fear." And after a moment, she added, "Not just for me. For everyone on Earth."

God smiled. "I think you have Me wrong, My dear. We do not sell fruits here. Only seeds."

We know that the seeds of change are in Radical Loving and Awesome Holiness. We know that the Love and Holiness we send out from our hearts can enter into the hearts of men and women, and especially the little children, all over this country and all over the world.

YOU ARE A PROPHET

How do we turn all these great and worthy aspirations into Earth-life reality?

How does God's message of love and holiness come into our world?

Just like the biblical prophets of ancient times, *you are a Prophet*.

You stand at the bush, atop the mountain, in the sheltering cleft of the Rock, in the cave, at the foot of the Temple, in the stream of exile and return.

You can hear, see, envision, daydream, and night-dream God.

God can and will give you messages.

Sometimes the message will be just for you or for you and your family.

At other times, God will give you a message that you are to give over to the world.

You are a Vessel and a Channel of the Holy Spirit.

God's continuing revelation lives in you.

You are a Prophet—receiving and transmitting the word of God.

Be assured: While it may seem overwhelming and even frightening to be in direct and intimate communication with God, and to be given an assignment like this by God, it is also very honoring, and good, and sweet. God has chosen you, and you have a wondrous, sacred task.

Also, be assured that God will never, ever give you a message that will be harmful to you or to anyone who hears you convey the transmission.

Sometimes people think that what they have heard, seen, or dreamed from God is good for them and will exclude, dismiss, belittle, debase, or eliminate other people or groups.

Never.

God loves all God's children equally.

God would never give either a warning or an inspiration to one over another. God would never choose one over another. Any chosen-ness is for responsibility, not superiority.

God's messenger—you—is chosen not to flaunt your relationship but to fulfill a holy mission. Your intimacy with God is never to be used for evil or to bring physical, emotional, or spiritual pain, suffering, or overlording. It is to be used for the greatest good of the Earth and all humankind.

Since prophecy and being a prophet may be new to you—and breathtaking, mind-blowing, and awesome—here is a little prayer that you can recite:

God,

Please:
Attune my hearing,
so that You can speak to me.
Sharpen my seeing,
so that You can show me.
Hone my senses,
so that You can dream into me by day and by night.
Let me be ever open and ever ready,
so that You can inspirit me.
Let me be a channel,
so that You can flow through me.

If you recite this meditation each day, you will grow in your ability to hear God speaking to you in the soft murmuring sound, the faint sound of a quiet whisper, the sound of delicate silence. You will be able see the visions that God puts before you and the dreams that God puts into you.

You are a Prophet.

THE ETERNAL SOUL

No matter how much we love, no matter how holy our words and deeds, no matter how great our contribution to the collective wisdom of the world or to creating a just and peaceful existence, no matter how much we cherish this life and want to be here—one day, each and every one of us is going to leave this Earth. We are, in common parlance, going to die.

> *A tourist visited a venerable sage. He was astonished to see that the sage's home was only a simple room filled with books. The only furniture was a table and a bench.*
> *"Where is your furniture?" asked the tourist.*
> *"Where is yours?" replied the sage.*
> *"Mine?" I am only a visitor here."*
> *The sage replied, "So am I."[1]*

For some, the Earth exit is blessed relief from the pain and anguish of physical illness or emotional distress. For some, it is good to leave this Earth's vale of tears, with all its problems, afflictions, and enigmas.

For most, it is a sad and sorrowful leave-taking because this world in which we have lived is filled with such beauty and magnificence. Our lives and our relationships have been so loving, so bountiful, so satisfying. We are reluctant to leave those whom we love so much, and we are brokenhearted that they will be bereft and left alone when we go on to the Great Beyond.

Our human emotions, and those of our dearest loved ones and friends, rightly bring tears, sobs, and wails of grief. Those who mourn for us feel lost and empty, and sometimes abandoned or angry, and experience waves of unspeakable sadness and despair. We and the ones we love intensely lament the loss of our physical presence, our bodies, the fragile vessels that have housed our souls for this brief sojourn on Earth.

Our profound distress, real and fervent, can be softened by our recognition of the limitations of Earthbound existence and Earthbound knowledge. We do not and cannot know the answers to the perplexing mysteries of life and death.

But our consternation can be tempered by the sage who teaches us, "Fear not death. It is just a matter of going from one room to the other."[2] In the deepest place, each of us—each God-created human being—knows our origins, our pathways, our destination. "How body from spirit does slowly unwind/Until we are pure spirit at the end."[3]

"Death is not the end; the earthly body vanishes; the immortal soul lives with God."[4] Our souls are eternal. When we are not here, we are present elsewhere. In whatever place and whatever form, the soul, the spirit, lives on forever.

The veil between This Side and The Other Side is becoming thinner and more permeable. The boundaries and the barriers are slowly melting. We are becoming more aware, more conscious. The sense of separation is falling away and we are feeling more and more of the connection, the wholeness, of All That Is. Soul-Energy ever endures. Our eternal souls are Home with God—where it is good, and sweet, and safe. We are the Oneness. We are the ever-continuing recipients of the gift of unending love.

> The Psalmist said: "You shall be happy, and it shall be good for you."
> The sages explain: "You shall be happy—in This World.
> "And it shall be good for you—in the World To Come."[5]

God—who placed a precious, pure soul into each Earth-body—is eternal. Our souls—our exquisite souls, our supreme gift from God—are eternal.

God is Love. Our souls are Love. Love has no limitation in time or space.

With God—in God's loving care—our souls never die. Our Love lives on forever and ever and ever.

From God.

To God.

In the Light of God.

The circle is never-ending.

The circle continues still.

In our Souls is Life Eternal

In our Souls is Eternal Life

Here.

There.

Now.

Always.

RIGHT NOW

We have articulated the sad and painful price that we and our world are paying for getting stuck in the old patterns of indifference and inaction.

Right now—before it is too late and before we lose our chance— the swirling turmoil in our world compels us to become the people who will tame and heal the darkness that threatens us.

Disaster and upheaval serve in part to purge and purify the old design. But more, they are cracking open our hearts. For, sometimes, when we experience our own suffering or the anguish of others, our hearts open wide to hold the pain and help as best as we can.

Yet when the present challenge or danger seems to have passed, instead of staying fully open and big-hearted, all too often our hearts close again and return to their "normal" size. We turn back to the details of our own lives—until the next event occurs to crack open our hearts again.

In today's world, when one painful event seems to follow another at warp speed, the message for us is: we need to keep our hearts open all the time. With open hearts we can carve out the pathways that revive and renew us so that the new paradigms can emerge.

Have you ever watched a chick hatch itself from its egg? That chick uses every bit of strength he possesses to peck a tiny hole in his shell. And he keeps pecking and moving and pecking some more— until he is completely free from his shell—no matter how long it takes or how exhausted he becomes in the process. The chick has no choice—he will die if he stays in his shell one moment longer.

Pecking his way out of his shell is the first thing that chick ever does—and it is the hardest thing he will ever do—and during that exhausting process, he doesn't know if he will survive it. But he clearly knows that if he stays where he is, he will definitely die. It is pure Faith and clear knowing that keeps him pecking.

It is time, Dearest Humans, for you to crack open your hearts. It is time for you to free your hearts from the hard shells that have kept them shielded and protected. It is the hardest, scariest thing you will ever do. It is the most exhausting endeavor of your lives—and you wonder whether you will survive the process.

It is Faith that gives you the strength and courage to survive the cracking open of your hearts. You have been working on building Faith, on learning to cling to the Divine for a long time. It is because Faith ... allows you to let go of your shells.[1]

When our hearts crack open, we become so very, very vulnerable. The armor in which we may have cloaked ourselves to protect our fragile small-self egos falls away, and we stand emotionally and spiritually naked.

The only way to survive is to grab onto God and hang on tight. Holding the Immense Expansiveness of the Divine requires us to give up our small selves on the promise that we each will feel part of the greater Self. That is called Faith.

As human beings, we are hard-wired to watch out for danger and always try to protect ourselves from peril. But when we are on constant watch for danger, what we are really doing is inviting it in. In this coming new age, a time when the Light of God shines more and more brightly, if our hearts remain armored, we will "get cooked" inside that armor.

What if there were no limitations to our love? What if we simply love? What if all the barriers come down and Divine Love just pours through us into every moment and every space? What if we let go and open our hearts so that love flows, and our world is filled with love and light, kindness, compassion and truth?

It would be the dawning of the new Eden on Earth!

The choice is ours. Will we remain small, or will we grow into our Divinity?

Since there is nothing that is outside of God, everything is a manifestation of God. All of creation is God expressing God. God is "Godding." And everyone and everything is being "Godded" at every moment.[2]

Every moment we choose to recognize the Presence of Divinity before us—in a person, a group, a plant, an animal, a crystal, a sound, an event, an unfolding in ourselves, and in our own reactions and responses—the love flows and the New Day becomes.

> *"Excuse me," said an ocean fish, "you are older than I, so can you tell me where to find this thing they call the ocean?"*
> *"The ocean," said the other fish, "is the thing you are in now."*
> *"Oh, this? But this is water. What I am seeking is the ocean,"*
> *said the disappointed fish as he swam away to search elsewhere.*

There isn't anything to look *for*. All we have to do is *look*. When we are aware enough, conscious enough, we can and will realize that God is manifesting in everyone and everything. And when we run into the Divine, our only possible response is Love. We fall into God's Heart.

What is the way into God's Heart? We come to God through our own hearts—our hearts that need to be heart-to-heart with God.

That is why our hearts must be cracked open now. Those who are in the process of cracking open hearts right now know how exhilarating and terrifying, joyful, despairing, and hopeful it is—all at the same time. It is literally *heartbreaking* to break through our heart's armor, and it is grievous and shattering to die to our small selves on a promise—on Faith that a greater Me will arise.

As we begin cracking open our hearts, as Love begins to flow through us, we re-member times when we've done this before, when we let ourSelves fall in love. So, thanks to the magic of social media, many are now reaching out to find old friends and lovers in order to recollect the sweetness and remember how we felt falling in love before. It is a bittersweet reminder of how we have had the daring courage to die to our small selves in order to be reborn a larger, greater Me.

As our hearts crack open, we recognize the Divinity all around, and we fall in Love with God. Then the vibration rises and more Light comes into our world.

And whenever there is more Light, the dark rises to the surface for healing and transformation. There will continue to be confusion and pain, yet this provides us the opportunity to practice recognizing, embracing, and expanding the Divinity inherent in each one; to love without limit.

The new Light fills in all the places and spaces, and opens us to see more and more of the Divine though Radical Loving and Awesome Holiness, the Oneness of All That Is.[3]

WHO ARE WE?

In the old movie *Wayne's World* (but not named for me) a character insists, "We're not worthy. We're not worthy." That is how so many of us feel: we're not worthy. Who are we to be charged with the tremendous task of bringing Light, and Love, and Holiness into our world? Who are we that we can be God's Heart and Hands on Earth? Who are we to be the messengers of the Divine, the instruments of the revolutionary transformation of humankind?

The Bible tells us We are the vessels through which God comes to Earth. At our deepest places, we know what is true and right and good; we know the power of Love, the majesty of Holiness. We know that we are God's partners. As much as we need God, God needs us.

> *You are My witnesses ... I Am God.*
> *When you are My witnesses, I Am God.*
> *When you are not My witnesses, I Am,*
> *as it were, not God.* (Midrash Tehillim 123:2 on Isa. 43:12)

How do we witness God?
How do we acknowledge God as God?
How do we give God place in our world, in our lives?
The Psalms teach:

> *In the morning my prayer comes before You* (Ps. 88:13).
> *So, it is said: "The angel who is in charge of prayer waits until all God's children on Earth have finished their prayers. Then the angel takes all the prayers and weaves them into a crown, and places the crown on God's head."* (Midrash Ps. 88:4)

We crown God. It is our prayer—our intimate conversations with the Divine, our fervent embrace, and our humble affirmation—that recognizes and accepts God as God on this precious Earth. Without us, our Earth is a magnificent but empty playground for God. With us, God has Earthly purpose, honor, and glory.

So, God and we meet.

> *Sinai is ever-present; not only a past event.*
> *Wherever people gather to seek God's Presence,*
> *To renew the covenant, to discover God's will,*
> *Whenever we listen and hear, receive and transmit,*
> *We stand at Sinai.*[1]

And God declares us most worthy to be the catalysts who will bring the messianic time of goodwill and peace to our world.

Lest we forget who we are and what a vital role we have in healing and perfecting our lives, an old story reminds us:

> *High in the mountains was a monastery that had once been known throughout the world. The monks who lived there were spiritual seekers; the people who came on retreat were enthusiastic. The chanting and praying and meditating deeply touched the hearts of all who came.*
>
> *But something had changed. Fewer and fewer people came to join the order; fewer and fewer people came for spiritual nourishment. Those who remained were disheartened and sad.*
>
> *Deeply worried, the Abbot went off in search of an answer. Why had his monastery fallen on such hard times? The Abbot came to the old sage and asked, "Is it because of some fault of ours, some sin of ours, that our monastery has fallen on such hard times?"*
>
> *"Yes," replied the sage. "It is because of the sin of ignorance."*
>
> *"The sin of ignorance?" questioned the Abbot. "Of what are we ignorant?"*
>
> *The sage looked at the Abbot for a long time and then said,*

"One of you is the Messiah in disguise. But of this you are all igno-rant." The sage was then silent.

"The Messiah?" thought the Abbot. "The Messiah—one of us? Impossible." But the sage had spoken. And so, traveling home, the Abbot considered: Who could it be? Is it Brother Cook? Is it Sister Vegetable Grower? Is it Brother Treasurer? Is it Sister Bell-Ringer? Which one? Which one? We all have our faults, our flaws, our failings. Isn't the messiah supposed to be perfect? Which one? Which one?

When the Abbot returned to the monastery, all the brothers and sisters gathered around, and the Abbot told them what the sage had said.

"One of us? The Messiah? Impossible."

But the sage had spoken, and the sage was never wrong.

One of us? The Messiah? Incredible! But it must be so. Which one? Which one? That brother over there? That sister? That one? Which one? Which one?

Whomever was the Messiah was surely in disguise. So, not know-ing who amongst them was the Messiah, they all began treating each other with new respect. Their words were sweeter; their actions toward each other were kinder. You never know, each one thought. He might be the one; she might be the one. I had better treat each and every one with decency and dignity, with grace and honor.

And the monastery was filled with newfound light, and sweet-ness and joy. Soon, new people came to live and learn there; people came from far and wide to be inspired by the smiles and the kind-ness that filled the monastery. Even the vegetables tasted better, and the bells seemed to sound happier.

For once again, the monastery was filled with the spirit of Love.

We may be hiding—even from ourselves—
but the happy and absolute truth of our lives is:

Each one of us is the Messiah.

God is Love.
    We are Love.
God is Holy.
    We are Holy.

          We are Your people.
          And You are our God.

BACK ON THE BENCH

We hear a Voice. It calls out to us from the Heavens and reverberates around the world. "My precious children. Please come. Meet Me in the Garden at our usual spot."

We gather from the four corners of the Earth, and when we arrive, there—sitting on our favorite bench holding Fido on a leash—is God.

"Hello, My dearest Ones. Thank you for coming."

"Good evening, God. We're so glad to see You. Thank You for inviting us. And it is great to see Fido, too."

Fido's tail wags in happy greeting, and God says, "Well, you must be wondering why I called you here."

We are, of course, a bit apprehensive. Is it good news? Bad news? Earth-shattering news? Just a friendly visit? Why has God called us back to the bench?

"Sure," we say. "Anytime You want to chat, we're very happy. And, of course, we are wondering what You want to tell us."

"Well," says God, "I've been listening and watching very carefully as you have received the design and the recipe for how to make our world a better place. And I see how you are opening your hearts to what is right and what is good.

"Still, there is far too much indifference. I weep when any one of My children goes hungry, or has no place to live, or goes unschooled. I weep every time one of My children harms another. There is still too much hatred. And there is far, far too much killing.

"So, first, I tell you: Do whatever you must to end the fear, the violence, the murder. Rid yourselves of the plagues that batter and break you. Go far beyond the tired old responses and find new

Earth-solutions to the ills that beset you. It is no longer time to *restore*. It is no longer time to *reform*. It is even no longer time to *rejuvenate*. It is time to *renew*. Renew your lives. Renew your planet. Renew hope.

"You can do it. You can go beyond the narrowness and limitations of your Earth-minds and into the limitlessness of your hearts. Envision. Imagine. Dream. And then make it happen. You are the builders of our new world.

"And that is why I Am so happy to see so many of you waking up and coming into the Light, becoming infused with the Light and Love that I send into the world. You are becoming Light Workers who give Light and Love into the darkness, who put your Light and Love into the faces of others, who illumine our world with goodness. You are bringing Love and Holiness—Radical Loving and Awesome Holiness—into our world and you are filling many places and people with faith in the new day that is dawning."

A wide smile comes to God's face, and we cannot help but reflect that smile. We still have a long way to go, but God is telling us that our journey toward rebirth and renewal has begun. "Thank You, God. Thank You, God. Thank You, God," we gratefully and happily say.

"Thank *you,* My precious children. As you begin the renewal of our world, I renew the promise I made long ago: 'There *is* great hope for your future (Jer. 31:17).'"

With that, God gets up from the bench, wakes Fido from a doggie-nap, and says, "Keep up the good work, My dearest Ones. I'll be walking with you as you bring evermore Light and Love and Holiness into our world. And I'll be celebrating with you as you bring Sky Blue—that great and wondrous time when our entire world will be bathed in peace. Let the birthing begin."

IN US

So, if God tells us that there is so much hope for our future, that we are birthing a new world that will bring us newfound purpose and joy, why are so many of us still feeling so bewildered, so unsettled, so uncertain?

A good part of the serious problems and challenges our world faces is that, throughout history and certainly today, we have leaders who have not led us into the "Promised Land" of healing, harmony, and peace—but have led us astray into disarray, disorder, and turmoil.

It used to be that our community, political, and spiritual leaders were paradigms of wisdom who lived their values and manifested their principles. That is why it is said,

> *I did not go to the Master*
> *to hear his teachings.*
> *I went to the Master*
> *To watch him tie his shoes.*

Throughout history and now, some leaders have been well-meaning but inexperienced and incompetent. Others have violated and desecrated their obligations and responsibilities to their country and people while seeking their own self-aggrandizement, power, prestige, and wealth. Their hunger for personal gain and unquestioned fidelity has far outweighed their commitment to the common good.

When good and true leaders have risen up, and have understood the human longing for justice and righteousness, when they have uplifted the human spirit with their vision for equality, freedom, and love—all too often they have been summarily dismissed, personally attacked, demeaned, denigrated, and discredited—their personal integrity and honor, besmirched and ruined. And at the very worst, they have met the crucifier or the assassin's bullet.

Today, we have twenty-first-century leaders who are trying to administer affairs of state through documents that are centuries-old, and to fulfill roles that are far too big for any one person. Even our spiritual guides and leaders are floundering as the world crumbles around us, and the old forms no longer bring the kind of comfort or inspiration that they once did.

Yet these are the very people we depend on to lead our communities and our countries—and, thus, our whole world—and to strive for the very best way of life for us and our children.

There is only one conclusion. We are counting on the wrong people and the wrong modes of leadership.

> *A Zen student, hoping to become a teacher, studied with the Master for ten years. After this time of apprenticeship, he felt ready to teach.*
>
> *The young student came to the Master for his blessing. It was a rainy day, so the student left his clogs and umbrella outside. The student said, "Master, I am ready to teach, and I have come for your blessing."*
>
> *The Master asked, "Did you leave your clogs and umbrella outside?"*
>
> *"Yes," the student replied.*
>
> *"Did you place your umbrella to the right or to the left of your clogs"*
>
> *The student stood confused and flushed, for he could not remember.*
>
> *And the Master said, "The time of learning has not ended."*

Our leaders need to be aware, constantly aware. And they need to be conscious, constantly conscious. Our leaders need to be wise and discerning. From where does awareness come? From where does wisdom and discernment come?

The Voice resonates and holds us.

> *Surely the Instruction that I give to you today is not too baffling for you, nor is it beyond your reach. It is not in the Heavens that you should say, "Who among us can go up to the Heavens and get it for us ...?" Neither is it across the sea, that you should say, "Who among us can cross to the other side of the sea, and get it for us ...." No. The thing is very close to you, in your mouth and in your heart .... I set before you this day, life and prosperity, death and adversity .... Choose life.* (Deut. 30:11–19)

Everything we need to live and to prosper, to feel happiness and satisfaction, is not outside of us. It is right within us—in the inner reaches of our hearts and our souls. We each have a Voice Within—a Voice that echoes from the beginning before the beginning, that knows beyond knowing, that understands the mysteries of the universe, that holds the formula for a world of goodness, and love, and peace.

Our task and our great privilege is to listen, listen, listen to that Inner Voice, to heed its lessons and to share and interconnect its message with the Voices Within of each and every other human being. Successful leadership is not imposed from the outside but grows and flourishes and is eventually articulated from deep inside. We can be like this shepherd of sheep:

> *A shepherd was tending his sheep close by a beautiful green meadow, near a sparkling spring. He feared that a wolf might come and snatch away his sheep, so he resolved to keep a most watchful eye.*
>
> *But, at nightfall, growing very tired, he lay down on the ground and fell asleep. Near midnight, he awoke with a start. He was immediately afraid, for he had never before fallen asleep watching over his sheep.*

He rushed to them, lying in the meadow, and saw them crowded up against one another. He counted them, and none was missing.

He cried out, "Dear God, how can I ever repay You? Entrust your sheep to me once more, and never again shall I neglect them. I will guard them with my life."

The caution, of course, is that some will claim: My Inner Voice is better than yours. My Inner Voice is truer than yours. My hearing of God's word and will is far greater than yours. My leadership is superior to yours. That is the flawed model that has brought anguish and suffering to our world far too often.

It is hard. True leadership can be complicated and messy. Accepting opposing points of view can be galling. Dealing with difficult personalities can be confounding. Respecting insufferable rants and outrageous behaviors can be painful. Mediating conflict can be arduous. Finding consensus can sometimes seem impossible. Weaving together a sense of Oneness can sometimes seem unimaginable.

True leadership is sourced not in political expediency, personal gain, or shameless demand. True leadership is sourced in God's Truth of the common good, the highest good, the greatest good for all God's children.

The birthing of a new world depends on our willingness and ability to listen to eternal wisdom, to experience enlightenment, to step forward to accept the mantle of leadership; to be like Joshua-of-old, who was able to succeed the incomparable Moses because he was filled with wisdom and the spirit of God.

True leadership interweaves all the thinking, feeling, spirit, and love of each and every person on this Earth who listens to the Inner Voice and who hears that voice giving its most potent and profound message: *See the Face of God in the face of every human being. Love, love, love. Live and Be Radical Loving and Awesome Holiness.*

Do you still think you are unprepared or unworthy to listen and to do?

Then speak and act "as if"—*as if* your actions make a difference, *as if* your words bring wisdom, *as if* real change can come about through the work of your hands, *as if* the love that flows from your heart enters into other hearts. And soon you will find that what you do and say has become very, very real.

Please remember that everything you need is within you, and you can do this!

> *Once a young artist shoved aside a block of marble as useless. The great Michelangelo said, "Bring that to my studio. An angel is imprisoned in that marble and I intend to set it free."*

So, as did the prophet of old, when God asks:

"Whom shall I send? Who shall go for us?"

our only possible reply can be:

"Here I Am. Send me." (Isa. 6:8)

With confidence, pride, and overflowing love, we are now ready to birth the new world—ours and God's.

BIRTHING OUR NEW WORLD

To bring our New World of Radical Loving and Awesome Holiness into Being, we can recite this invocation.

> *The world is co-created as we breathe—*
> *Let us Live Larger.*
> *Let us Dream Vividly.*
> *Let us Be Now.*
> *We now have 100 percent desire for all to prosper and delight*
> *in Love and Peace!*
> *The world is co-created, as we are—*
> *Let us Be Oneness.*[1]

YES . . . AND:
A PERSONAL WORD

Even with hearing directly from God, even hearing God's stirring call to rebirth and renewal, even with knowing that the capacity for Radical Loving and Awesome Holiness is right inside us, I expect that there can and will be objection to (almost) everything I have said here.

I will be accused of being misinformed or uninformed; naïve or foolish; too partisan or not partisan enough; too faith-based or not faithful enough; too fear-based or not fearful enough. I will also be accused of blurring the boundaries of politics, personalities, social policy, national interests, and religion; of being too painfully realistic, or of having delusional utopian fantasies.

And to (almost) every objection, counter-argument, and passionate disagreement—regardless of how varied and disparate the arguments may be—my response is (almost) always the same: "You are right."

You are right. In this little book, I have made statements that are stark and steadfast, and leave little room for equivocation. Why? I am pained and terrified by what is happening in our world right now.

I respect and honor each person's right to choose a life-view and life-action. But I sadly conclude that too much of what is being chosen these days is not right.

Indeed, so much of what is being chosen is very, very wrong. And I know that so many of the choices that are being made are leading our world to the brink of disaster.

Old, tired ideas and behaviors that are deeply ingrained and comfortable are all too often ineffective and unproductive. And very often,

YES . . . AND: A PERSONAL WORD

they have been harmful. I ask: Over the years, over the centuries, where has this old insular thinking, these old self-serving actions, gotten us?

They have not stopped the enmity. They have, instead, increased the hatred, bigotry, racism, nationalism, wars, and weapons that have poisoned the world with fear and loathing and filled the cemeteries of our countries with the fair youth of our lands.

They have not stopped the competitive rivalries. They have, instead, increased the greed, arrogance, and lust for power of flawed and dangerous people who, despite their most fervent attempts at domination, may have only shifted a border, or gained temporary political rule, or filled a treasury now and then.

It is true. Charismatic men and women have their shining moments upon the world stage—and so often cause untold damage and destruction. "If we do not remember history, are we doomed to repeat it?"[1] We cannot possibly again permit self-centered, cunning individuals with despoiled egos to wreak havoc on our fragile world. Now—as it has been in the past—their tales, full of sound and fury, ultimately signify nothing of worth. They must be heard no more.

I am sorry if I sound harsh.

I am sorry if I seemingly easily dismiss opposition.

But we cannot—*we cannot*—ignore the very real threats that hang over us. We have to act—with swiftness, with absolute resolve, with abiding passion.

I am haunted by the words of the Reverend Dr. Martin Luther King Jr. *zt"l* in his Lenten sermon at the National Cathedral in Washington, DC on March 31, 1968.

> *One day we will have to stand before the God of history and we will talk in terms of things we have done. Yes, we will be able to say we have built gargantuan bridges to span the seas, we have built gigantic buildings to kiss the skies. Yes, we have made our submarines to penetrate oceanic depths. We have brought into*

being many other things with our scientific and technological power.

It seems that I can hear the God of history saying, "That was not enough! But I was hungry, and ye fed me not. I was naked and ye clothed me not. I was devoid of a decent sanitary house to live in, and ye provided no shelter for me. And consequently you cannot enter the kingdom of greatness. If ye do it unto the least of these my brethren, ye do it unto me." That is the question facing America today.

Only five days later, Dr. King was assassinated. His resolute voice and urgent message were stilled. And now, more than fifty years later, his prophetic call for a just and good society has yet to be fulfilled.

There is no more time to wait.

The concepts offered here—as they have throughout the history of humankind—hold the Divine Design for all of us. They envision nothing less than building our own lives and our whole world on human and civil rights, goodness, righteousness, justice, decency, dignity, kindness, and compassion for every person on this Earth.

All we have to do is embrace this vison, commit to it, and make it happen. As the esteemed late war hero Senator John McCain put it: "There is nothing more liberating than to fight for a cause larger than yourself, something that encompasses you but is not defined by your existence alone."

At our peril, we have ignored Love and Holiness for too long.

No matter how elusive it may seem, no matter how hard it feels to achieve:

Love is our only hope for salvation.
Holiness is our only pathway to redemption.
Radical Loving.
Awesome Holiness.
Now.

THE SPIRIT IS UPON US

A Prayer and a Blessing

From the beginning ...
    from before the beginning of the beginning ...
    we've been waiting.
From time before time and for all these eons ...
    we've been waiting.
And God has been waiting too.
We've been waiting for this exact moment ...
    for this uncovering, this unfolding, this new beginning.
And now the time has come.

We who stand at the precipice embrace the revelation.
The spirit of Source descends upon us, and we rise up in response.
The call comes, and we ascend to embrace.
We are children of the universe.
We are children of God.
We are God's co-creative partners in the ongoing process
    of genesis ever-renewed.

The Name of God has been spoken.
Our summons echoes from the primordial soup, through the
    heights of Sinai, through the Cross and the Crescent, through
    the Om and the Bodhi.

Open to us, O, God, and we promise, we will open to You.
Return us unto You, and we promise, we will return.

We will heal the world from her pain and perfect the world from
   her brokenness.

We will weave the Tree of Life and Knowledge with our prayers and
   meditations, our good works and righteous deeds.
We will bring transformation and evolution.
Old hatreds will cease; old enemies will lay down their tools of war.
We will fashion a world of unity, harmony, and love.
Brothers and sisters of humankind will touch hands in peace.

The long wait is over.
The dawn-light of this new age breaks forth.
One God. One World. One People.

In the Heavens and on Earth,
In the Heart of Hearts,
And in the Soul of Souls,
In the ever-continuing journey back to Eden,
In life and in life-everlasting,
The circle is never-ending,
The circle continues still.
From God,
To God.
Forever with God.

Only one thing do we ask.
This do we desire:
Bless us, O God ...
Please bless us
   with the Light of Your Holy Presence,
   and under the wings of Your enduring Love.

      And may we, we pray,
      Be a blessing to You.

                    Amen. Amen.

AND WE ALL SAY

Imagine

Envision

Create

ONE GOD

ONE WORLD

ONE PEOPLE

*

ONE GOD

ONE WORLD

ONE PEOPLE UNITED IN LOVE

Namaste:
    Let the Divine in me see the Divine in you.
    Let the Divine in you see the Divine in me.
We can love God and each other—passionately, radically.
We can be holy—intensely, awesomely.
We can join hands and hearts to save ourSelves and to redeem our world.

The work goes on,
the cause endures,
the hope still lives,
and the dream shall never die."[1]

We *will* bring

RADICAL LOVING

and

AWESOME HOLINESS

We *will* bring

EDEN ON EARTH

AFTERWORD

I wrote *Radical Loving* as an aspirational vision—a hard, candid look at our world as it is and a fervent hope for what it can be.

It was my cry of bewilderment and pain at all that separates us, and at the bigotry, demagoguery, and provocations that fuel our divisions. It was a call to move away from the selfish egoism, narcissism, racism, misogyny, homophobia, xenophobia, Islamophobia, and anti-Semitism that plague and rot our society.

Not only were we not moving in the right direction, but in many ways our lives were getting worse. Our differences and conflicts were being exacerbated by inept, incompetent, self-aggrandizing, so-called governmental "leadership." Day by day, the societal dilemmas on which this book originally focused were playing out before our eyes. We and our institutions were being split apart by selfishness and self-interest. We were losing our core principles of equality and justice, of striving for the common good. Our own pocketbooks and pleasures took precedence over compassion and love. Faith was overcome by fear.

In our distress, the cry of the prophet-of-old began ringing in our ears, "Awake! Awake! Arise! Shake off the dust!" (Isa. 52:1, 3). And we heard the knocking on our doors, "Get up! Get up! Do the work of the Creator!" Now. Before it is too late.

So, *Radical Loving* was a plea—and a practical design—to see the God-spark in ourselves and each other; to embrace the age-old dream of Oneness that could finally come to be in our day.

Could we take the leap from theory to practical action?

The political process began its slow, arduous slog toward change and renewal.

Our own instincts for self-survival and a meaningful existence began to stir.

And then.

Our vision was smacked by real-life events.

Our world exploded with a virulent virus—an honest-to-goodness medical plague that swept the globe, sickened millions, killed hundreds of thousands, and sent humankind into forced quarantine in a valiant attempt to save lives. Coronavirus—known as COVID-19—became a planetary pandemic.

We watched in horror as the number of cases and the death tolls mounted. We saw reports of overloaded hospitals, overworked medical professionals, underequipped medical facilities. We were dumbfounded when temporary hospital tents were set up in public parks and refrigerated trucks were brought in to be temporary morgues to hold the dead. Our world, our way of life, was turned topsy-turvy, and all we could do was stand witness in stunned silence and hope against hope that we did not become infected.

Almost immediately, our true natures were on worldwide display.

In the places where government leaders heeded medical and scientific counsel and imposed the most stringent steps to protect the populace, the dread disease—still bringing with it much pain and many fatalities—was somewhat corralled and diminished. While there was no cure, there was mitigation. Doctors, nurses, first responders, and health-care professionals all risked their own lives and well-being to treat their very, very ill patients. They came out of deepest love and loyalty to their profession and to the ones who so desperately needed them. They are to be highly and humbly praised.

But in places—sadly, like the United States—where political agendas and ineptitude clashed with medical science, the pandemic ran wild. Its momentous danger was downplayed; sufficient critical medical equipment was not made available; likely defenses and deterrents were not strongly enacted. The wearing of masks and gloves, washing hands, and social distancing—all helpful strategies to keep the disease from spreading from person to person—were considered by many people as voluntary but not compulsory. The stay-inside "shutdown" or "lockdown" had some effect, but too many ignored the mandates, considering them too onerous, too much an impingement on individual freedoms—especially when they had such grave consequences for the admittedly horrible economic impact for the nation, for small businesses, and for wage-earners and their families.

The stay-at-home shutdown was hard—very hard. We are social beings, and in an instant our usual interaction with other people stopped. No gathering at work, at meetings, at parties, at church, mosque, or synagogue. No handshakes, no hugs; six-foot distancing from each other when we went outside for what was called "essential services"—a doctor's appointment, grocery shopping. There was a very real sense of isolation and aloneness, loss and grief, that encircled the planet.

Still, it can be said that the shutdown had some very positive aspects. Instead of being inundated with daily pollution, the Earth Herself began to breathe again. Smog blew away, and instead of being able to see for blocks, we could see for miles. Animals began to reclaim land that was once theirs. It may have been frightening to see mountain lions walking the streets of Los Angeles, and it was strange to see dolphins swimming in the canals of Venice where the gondolas had recently been floating. But it reminded us that we are but visitors on this pure Earth, and that we and our animal friends need to find ways to live in harmony again.

With people in isolation, the fast-paced world which we had created slowed down. We will never know if it was serendipity or if it was the Divine plan to prepare us for this time: only a few decades ago, we began to make personal computers, and tablets, and the Internet, and smartphones. With these blessed devices, we began to really connect with each other in deep ways once again. Thank you, Skype and Zoom, and Facetime, Instagram, and Twitter—and myriad other technological gifts that keep us emotionally and spiritually together even when we have to be physically apart.

It was heart-wrenching when we could not be in the hospitals with our loved ones when they were ill and dying, and that they had to die alone without our loving presence, and that we had to let them go without a final kiss. And it was so painful when only a very few people could attend funerals, denying the deceased the honorific accompaniment to the grave and the outpouring tributes they deserved. And it was sad when the festivities for graduations, and weddings and Bar Mitzvahs, and First Holy Communions were delimited and quiet, taking place without the scores of guests who would have been invited to celebrate.

Yet, the unexpected bonus of having connecting-technology was that people who might not be able to be together because of distance or available time or money, were able to gather "virtually" for these life-events. Old friends who had lost touch found each other again on social media. Here at home, and in countries around the world, people found unique ways to be together: they stood outside to cheer for the doctors and nurses and medical personnel. Musicians played their instruments and sang their songs for neighbors to hear. Worshippers stood outside their own homes to gather together in prayer. People organized "drive-by" events to acknowledge and celebrate birthdays, anniversaries, and especially, graduations. Out of separation, new connections were born.

In our most intimate relationships, we learned to renew love through kindness, patience, and self-sacrifice. The old joke is that when the husband retired from his long-time job, his wife was asked how his retirement was going for them as a couple. She replied, "I married him for better or for worse, but not for lunch." The current COVID joke is that nine months from now, the two most busy professions will be midwives and divorce attorneys.

The isolation was most difficult for people who live alone, who had no one for conversation, shared meals, intimacy. "The hardest part of this whole experience," more than one person reported, "is that I have not touched another human being, or been touched by another human being in all these months".

This pandemic can teach us one of life's most important lessons. No matter how vital we thought our jobs, our professions, our achievements, our resources, our possessions—what is at the core of our beings is our desire, our need, to love and be loved.

And we were all starkly reminded that nothing that is "outside" is as important as what is "inside." The strength of our inner selves, our character, our emotional and spiritual strength was sorely tested. And we were intensely reminded that true equanimity and assurance comes from the absolute knowing that the Divine is our center and our security. The pandemic intensified our hunger for the Divine, for we know that despite any and all of the challenges of the temporal world, when we stay deeply connected to God, existential angst and loneliness fade away—for together with God, we *can* face and overcome anything and everything.

With our children out of their classrooms, and parents called on to supervise and add to their children's distance learning, we all learned what precious and difficult tasks teachers have in educating our young ones. We owe much more gratitude and recompense to our middle school teachers than to our baseball middle infielders.

And with our children out of their classrooms there is this macabre reality: there was not a school-shooting in America. A blessing in disguise? Yes. A compelling call for immediate and fundamental change in how our children are protected, and surely, how the child-killers—who are so often mere children, themselves—must be stopped? Absolutely!

Yet, with America—and the world—devastated by the pandemic, there was great suffering in the land.

For so many businesses—from major corporations to mom-and-pop stores all around the country—the economy plunged very quickly. The economic circle shattered. The supply chain broke (most famously

for toilet paper), and millions and millions of people lost their jobs
and health insurance and applied for unemployment compensation.
Families were without income, food could not be purchased, rents
and mortgages could not be paid. The stock market and investment
portfolios rode a daily roller coaster. And we were starkly reminded
that the economy is not based on Wall Street for the few, but in the
local pizza parlor, the dry cleaners, the neighborhood restaurants, and
in the barbershops and hair salons. The government fumbled its way
in an attempt to help. But it was far too little and far too caught up
in political gamesmanship and favoritism. Food banks had to rise up
to feed the hungry, and shelters tried to find places for the homeless.
The situation was dire.

But no matter. Or very much mattered. Political expediency and
public pressure led to the so-called "re-opening" of public places. All
of a sudden, the deep conflicts that had fragmented America for so
long exploded in new frustration, controversy, hostility, confrontations, and altercations.

The age-old clash between individual rights and freedoms and the
highest common good played out in America's homes, schools, places
of worship, businesses, halls of government, and local street corners.

There were those who (seemingly so rightly for them) insisted that
the quarantine end so that they could reopen their businesses and
earn some income (limited though it might be) to feed their families.

And then there were also those who insisted that America reopen
so that they could go out for dinner, go to a bar to drink and dance, or
play at the beach.

Necessity versus personal desire.

Good cause versus good times.

Over and over again, the scientists and the medical professionals
told us that wearing face masks covering our noses and mouths could
and would reduce the spreading of the virus. Masks would protect us
from others and, more, protect others from us.

But, here again, the so-called political leadership failed us by denying the importance of masks. Instead of modeling mask-wearing, they gave tacit permission to be in public without a mask. Those who went maskless insisted that it was their "constitutional right" to exercise their individual freedom, even if it trampled on the highest common good. There seemed to be little concern for the well-being and lives of others.

These folks somehow conveniently forgot that the community sets rules to protect the rights and well-being of others, even at the expense of their individual freedoms. They stop at red lights—obviously curtailing their freedom to drive as they choose. They do not shout "Fire!" in a crowded theater—obviously curtailing their freedom to speak as they choose. They have to obtain a license to get married, drive a car, catch a fish, hunt, or run a business—obviously curtailing their freedom to do as they please anytime they please. All for the highest common good.

They never knew—or conveniently forgot—that during World War II the American government rationed food, encouraged the growing of "Freedom Gardens," had little children collecting aluminum cans and tin foil, and had everyone buying War Bonds—all to "help the war effort." Americans gladly made these sacrifices to support the highest good for the entire community.

But wear a mask to diminish the disease? No. No. Do not dare trample on my personal rights and freedom.

Once again: Necessity versus personal desire.

Good cause versus feeling good.

It was simple. In the places where people stayed at home and wore masks if they went out—often mandated by wise and caring governors and mayors—the number of cases and deaths went down. In places where people left home to gather—usually without masks—in crowded public places, the number of cases and deaths spiked higher and higher.

Prevention versus exposure.

Health versus illness.

Life versus death.

The question of reopening schools—from pre-school through university—was much more nuanced and complex. Surely, our young ones need to be educated, to keep up with their grade-level learning, to socialize and be socialized by interaction with their peer groups. Certainly, the best way to achieve those goals is in a school classroom with a trained professional teacher. But the virus quarantine took the children from their schoolrooms and kept them at home, with the hope that their education could be ongoing through online "distance learning" supervised and enhanced by their parents, grandparents, and guardians who had to help their children stay in school when there was no school to stay in.

The problem with that hope was multi-faceted: teachers with little knowledge about online education had much to learn and had to adapt their skills very rapidly. The learning curve for children and their parents to utilize online learning was steep and difficult. While children seem to have unlimited attention spans for computer games, they have far less patience for on-screen math and science. And most parents have little background in formal educational methodologies; they were ill equipped to immediately become effective teachers. For the upper-grade students, many parents who are expert in their own fields may have far less knowledge in their son or daughter's academic subjects. So their junior and senior high school students were not getting enough of the help they needed to keep up with their studies. And finally, many working parents were now working from home. It was very, very hard to keep up with a full-time job—especially when many of those parents were, themselves, learning new technologies necessary for their work—and at the same time supervise and assist with their children's school work. Add to this the family dynamic of the regular challenges of marriage and parenting, everyone being confined to home, the normal burden of housekeeping, and the additional burden of preparing every meal. Exhaustion, frustration, and continuing uncertainty about the future made the at-home learning environment far less than ideal.

Reopen the schools? Yes, some insisted—including high-ranking government officials, regardless of their qualifications to make such decisions. Learning must go on. Our children must continue to receive the very best education we can provide—and that is in a proper classroom setting.

Absolutely not, countered the medical and logistic experts. How is it possible to sanitize and keep safe the school facilities every day, every hour? How is it possible to keep all the children, teachers, administrators, and staff from contracting or spreading the dread disease? The risks are too great. How dare we expose our precious children to danger? What if—God forbid—little ones were to die from the virus that they contracted at school? How could this nation ever forgive itself?

Even if it is with the best intentions:
the insistence of the few versus the well-being of the many,
momentary satisfaction versus long-term favorable outcome?
Freedom without responsibility is no freedom at all.

And Then.

Another explosion.

In late May, in Minneapolis an innocent black man, George Floyd, was killed by a police officer who kept his knee on Floyd's neck for eight minutes and forty-six seconds while Floyd kept pleading, "I can't breathe. I can't breathe."

There are very fine, decent, well-intentioned, highly respected, community-minded law enforcement officers throughout the United States and around the world. But this particular policeman seemed to go beyond the bounds of his mandate to serve and protect. He was indicted for murder. But that legal action was nowhere enough for the citizenry of Minneapolis, both black and white and every shade in between, who took to the streets in passionate protest. Brokenhearted and angry, the protesters demanded an end to police brutality and justice for the slain man and his family. As street protests sometimes do, this one—which went on for many days—became violent itself, and led to looting and destruction of property. Law enforcement responded vigorously, and the cycle of brutality continued unbroken and unsolved.

The protests in Minneapolis led to similar outpourings in cities across the United States. The conscience of the country was aroused. The underlying systemic racism that has plagued America since its beginnings was unleased from its dark shadows and exposed in all its raw immorality.

The cry went up and became insistent: *Black Lives Matter*. It became a rallying cry, a plea of both desperation and aspiration. These words were painted on streets and buildings and embossed on T-shirts. The principle of the inherent worth of every black person is surely long overdue. The goal can no longer be "integration"; it must be full and unquestioned equality. Our world must become color blind.

There is, however, a caution: there are some within the Black Lives Matter movement who traffic in tropes of anti-Zionism and anti-Semitism. Discrimination is discrimination in any form and against any group. Those who call for equality and justice must advocate for every human being—regardless of race, color, creed, or religion. The house must always be clean in order for the cause to be pure.

To complicate already explosive conditions in the country, when the protests spread to Portland, Oregon, the president of the United States—without warning, and without the consent of the governor of the state or the mayor of the city—sent federal agents to the beleaguered metropolis. These troops were dressed in camouflage uniforms and were outfitted in full military protective gear. They wore neither badges nor name identification. They employed pepper spray, tear gas, and rubber bullets—even tear-gassing Portland's mayor, who was at a demonstration in sympathy with his citizens. They arrested demonstrators at will, put them into unmarked vehicles, and held them in undisclosed places. There was no way for attorneys to represent the detainees or invoke habeas corpus on their behalf, because no one could find them.

Without cause—except for his own self-declared definition of "law and order"—the president sent his personally ordered militia forces into the streets to behave like storm troopers—and threatened to send the troops to many other cities across the country. Many heard the echoes of a frightening not-too-distant past. Is this America? Or is it Nazi Germany? What is happening to our country?

It is true: justifiable protest demonstrations and movements are often infiltrated by agitators—many with their own nefarious agendas—coming from both the far right and the far left of the political spectrum. They obfuscate and sully the primary purpose of the protest and use their own urban guerilla tactics—often including gratuitous terror and violence—to jeopardize the integrity of the original cause. Their only intent is to advance their own political (most often anti-government) objectives. They are to be recognized for who and what they are, and opposed as an unwanted obstacle to the crucial issues being addressed with peaceful, non-violent protest.

As if all this were not enough to break the soul of a nation, then came Kenosha, Wisconsin. A black man, Jacob Blake, already restrained by law enforcement, was shot seven times in the back at point blank range by a police officer. Again, the protest demonstrations erupted— and again, the agitators, rioters, and looters took advantage of the uprisings to provoke and incite social unrest.

And again, the rhetoric that came from the highest levels of government was not of reconciliation and harmony, but of fomenting division and enflaming the worst human instincts.

Still, with all of this, men and women of good will—excepting, of course, the white supremacists, the skinheads, the America-Firsters, the fascists, the neo-Nazis, and the politicians who pander to their vile baseness—took up the cause. The names and memories of those who had been killed by police brutality around the country over the last few years were remembered and became part of the calls for racial equality. The advances that were legislated, particularly those beginning in the 1960s, were recalled and the lack of progress since then was lamented. Quickly, it became clear: if the United States is to continue to be the strong and visionary nation it once was and can be again, the long wait must end. Immediate and profound action must be taken to root out systemic racism so that the words, "liberty and justice for all" have real meaning that is felt and lived at the core of our beings.

That is why politicians must legislate—and they will. But the real change, the real affirmation of racial equality can only come from deep within individual hearts and souls.

In only a few months, all the issues raised here in *Radical Loving* were no longer theoretical or aspirational. They burst forth into the glaring reality of the everyday.

Will we continue the hatred, bigotry, greed, and selfishness that has plagued us for so long and has characterized so much of our existence in recent days?

Or will we begin to understand the absolute truism that to make America, and our whole world with us, truly great—is to know that "the only way to get it together is together"? Will we honor individual freedom and rights, *and* at the same time know at the deepest places in our beings that the only way we survive and flourish is to strive for the common good, the highest good, the greatest good?

In the ongoing saga of our world, this is a time for soul-reckoning:

Political and personal power and domination, or the cooperative saving of the entire body politic?

The pleasure of the moment, or the discipline of self-sacrifice?

Satisfying ego, or rising above self?

Fear or love?

Riding the higher vibration, or being left behind?

Sometimes a pandemic—no matter how devastating—is, well, just a pandemic. But sometimes—most times—it is an opening to a whole new way of being.

We stand at the crux of what was and what can and must be. In order for the new world to birth, the old world and its established institutions have to crumble. Nothing is or ever can be the same again—not government, politics, economics, business, work, education, medicine, science and technology, the environment, communication, religion, the arts, leisure, recreation, travel, personal care, intimate relationships, family, community. Everything—*everything*—will be different. This breaking precedes a massive breakthrough. Uncertain and painful though it may be, this enormous axial change is the beacon and the gateway to the unfolding redemption, evolution, and transformation of our universe.

When human beings see in each other the Face of God who created us all, we can enwrap each other in love and holiness.

> *Years ago, anthropologist Margaret Mead was asked by a student what she considered to be the first sign of civilization in a culture. The student expected Mead to talk about fishhooks, or clay pots, or grinding stones.*
>
> *But no. Mead said that the first sign of civilization in an ancient culture was a femur (thighbone) that had been broken and then healed. Mead explained that in the animal kingdom, if you break your leg, you die. You cannot run from danger, get to the river for a drink, or hunt for food. You are meat for prowling beasts. No animal survives a broken leg long enough for the bone to heal.*
>
> *A broken femur that has healed is evidence that someone has taken time to stay with the one who fell, has bound up the wound, has carried the person to safety, and has tended the person through recovery. Helping someone else through difficulty is where civilization starts.*

That is why Dr. Mead taught, "Never doubt that a small group of thoughtful, committed people can change the world. Indeed, it is the only thing that ever has."

Within each one of us is the power and the passion to renew our world.

Can we summon the determination and the courage to make the journey?

America can heal itself from the plagues of physical disease, a fractured social fabric, a broken moral compass, and widening spiritual malaise.

And the world can weave together a bright tapestry embodying the intrinsic values of freedom, equality, basic human and civil rights, justice, and dignity for every inhabitant of every nation on this Earth.

> An end to discrimination, and segregation, and self-proclaimed superiority.
>
> An end to terror and violence.
>
> An end to authoritarian brutality.
>
> An end to easy access to guns, and shooting deaths in our streets and schools.
>
> An end to raping our lands, polluting our skies, and despoiling our planet.
>
> An end to poverty, and hunger, and homelessness, and illiteracy.
>
> An end to the antagonisms between nations, and races, and religions, and ideologies, and genders.
>
> An end to political hypocrisy and corporate gluttony.
>
> An end to greed and avarice.
>
> An end to the lust for power and domination.
>
> An end to war and destruction.

And

> The embracing of awe.
>
> The embracing of gratitude.
>
> The embracing of human and civil rights.

The embracing of the wisdom of the past and the enlightenment of the future.

The embracing of decency and dignity, grace and goodness,
justice and righteousness, kindness and compassion.

The embracing of each other in light and love.

The embracing of the Divine.

The embracing of the vision and the promise of a world of
Oneness and peace.

The embracing of Radical Loving and Awesome Holiness.

Paraphrasing the Talmud: "There are singular moments in our lives
when we can discern the entire reason for our existence ..." (BT AZ,
10b).

Our time has come.

Our moment is now.

We have to be ready to fulfill our destiny.

We have to be joyfully willing to love, love, love.

The pandemic and the civil unrest have finally cracked open our
hearts. The light is slowly flowing in. We sense, we feel, we see, the
new world-home waiting for us to grasp it and step inside.

Home is in the heart of love.

And God is eagerly waiting to welcome us Home.

ACKNOWLEDGMENTS

Modeh Ani.

I am grateful.

Very, very grateful.

On Thanksgiving Day 2016 my wife Ellen and I were visiting in New York. We went to a kosher deli for a traditional turkey dinner.

Rather surprisingly, our waiter—who, knowing that we are Jewish because we were eating in his kosher restaurant and I was wearing a *kepa*, a Jewish head-covering—pulled up a chair, sat down at our table, and began speaking to us. He introduced himself as Mohammed, and identified himself as a Muslim.

After a few social niceties, he began an animated soliloquy that went on for more than ten minutes. He talked to us about the election of the new president of the United States and how afraid he and his family and his community are because of the president's positions on Muslims, travel, immigration, and deportation. He was concerned not only for himself but for the outrage against humanity that he believes the (then) president-elect's policies reflect. How, he asked, can the rainbow spectrum of humanity be lumped into solitary categories? Why, he asked, has our world become so dogmatic, narrow-minded, polarized, mean-spirited, and shrill?

Then, with great passion, he spoke about a world where people respect, befriend, and embrace each other despite differences in race, creed, ethnicity, religion, or culture. He was not at all self-serving but, rather, a human being who feels a kinship with all other human beings, all other children of God—regardless of how we each define

God. Rarely have Ellen and I heard such a simple, lucid expression of Oneness consciousness and sincere, heartfelt love.

In that moment, the idea for this book bubbled up inside me. Mohammed deserves a measured and serious response to his bewilderment and pain. So do all the rest of us who are struggling with the same issues and feel as if we are caught in the whirlwind of an existential crisis.

In many ways, *Radical Loving* is the capstone of all that I have been living, teaching, and writing through the decades of my life and rabbinate.

It is sourced in the Torah-based lessons of my childhood both from my parents, Hyman and Roberta Dosick *zt"l*—whose lives and memories remain a great blessing—and the synagogue of my youth, Congregation Rodfei Zedek in Chicago's multiracial, multiethnic Hyde Park neighborhood. It was honed by the prophetic sense of social justice that permeated the teachings at my seminary, the Hebrew Union College in Cincinnati. It is anchored in my formation and discernment, shaped in so many ways by the Cold War of the 1950s, the civil rights and antiwar movements and the feminist revolution of the sixties, and the struggle to Save Soviet Jewry of the late-sixties and early-seventies. It has been reinforced through my career-long work responding to the deepest needs of my people, my land, and my world, and by my ongoing pain—and shame—that there is even one person who is deemed "The Other," or one hungry or homeless, or unschooled, or poverty-stricken person on the face of this Earth.

I am guided by my teachers, both far and near in time and place, who helped shape my thinking and enflame my spirit. While there are far too many to name here, as you read in the chapter entitled "Lineage and Legacy," I give thanks to each them and still call upon their wisdom every day. Very special gratitude: to the teacher of my youth, Dr. Irving H. Skolnick; my "Reb School Rebbe," Rabbi Dr. Jakob J. Petuchowski *zt"l*; to the teachings of Rabbi Dr. Abraham Joshua

Heschel *zt"l*, and Elie Wiesel *zt"l* (to whom this book is dedicated); and to the Rebbe-visionaries of renewal in our generation, Rabbi Shlomo Carlebach *zt"l* and Rabbi Dr. Zalman Schachter-Shalomi *zt"l*.

As always, I am so very grateful to my longtime "kitchen cabinet" for their counsel, straight-talk advice, and confidence: Joseph (Yossi) Adler, Rabbi Samuel Barth, Dr. Steven R. Helfgot, and Alan M. Rubin. And my deepest gratitude goes out to my continuing mentors, my Spiritual Elders and *chevruta*: Rabbi Dr. Yehuda Shabatay, Rabbi Jack Riemer, Rabbi Dr. Jack Shechter, Rabbi Leah Novick; and "my priest," Fr. James J. O'Leary, S.J.; and, in Jerusalem, Rabbi Joe and Rolinda Schonwald, Rabbi Itzchak Evan Shayish, Rabbi Shlomo Katz, and Rabbi Sholom Brodt *zt"l*. With tears still in my eyes and deep sorrow in my heart, I honor the memory of my dear friend and colleague Rabbi Dr. David M. Posner *zt"l*, whose brilliant counsel and deep compassion would surely have been reflected in these pages, and who continues to teach from the World Beyond.

Unending gratitude to these additional friends and colleagues who read unfolding iterations of the manuscript, and offered their wise and keen commentary. They are children of spirit who are building a better world through their daily contributions to our ever-evolving world: my dear sister, Karen Dosick Grinfeld; my sister-in-law, Terry Kaufman; and Rabbi David Baron, Elisheva Baron, Cantor Susan Adler, Rabbi Marc Berkson, Annie Klein, Dr. Benjo Masilungan, Dr. Wayne Padover, Dr. Kim Rubinstein, Deni Phinney, Dr. Virginia Shabatay, June Carla Sinclair, and Elizabeth Wragee.

Deepest love and gratitude to my precious son, Seth, whose soul-wisdom and contemporary sensibilities bring balance to an "old man's" perspectives. And to our adored Anna and Jennifer to whom we can— *and must*—leave a better world.

I am so grateful to my students, especially the precious members and friends of The Elijah Minyan whom I am so privileged to serve, for their eagerness to engage and learn, and for their probing and challenging questions, which sharpen my thinking and gladden my heart.

Deepest thanks to the women and men—children of spirit, each and all—whose words of endorsement grace this book. They are giants in the World of Spirit; each in his or her own way shares and actively promotes the vision of Oneness for our world. Their faith in my articulation of our shared quest is one of the great honors of my life.

I am profoundly grateful to the amazing author and spiritual guide, Mirabai Starr—if you haven't yet, please read her books immediately; you will be enriched by her teachings and dazzled by her writing—for making the (re)connection for me with Paul Cohen, the incredible publisher of Monkfish Book Publishing. The motto of the company, "The Seeker's Press," tells all. This is a publishing house dedicated to bringing the World of Spirit into our lives. Founder and publisher Paul Cohen is the living embodiment of all that his company professes: he is a thinker and a feeler, a pragmatic practitioner and an inspirited visionary. And above all he is a real *mensch*—a gentleman and a gentle man of highest character and honor.

At Monkish is a wonderful staff of dedicated and enthused lovers of books of spirit. My deepest admiration and appreciation to Dory Mayo, the brilliant copyeditor, whose literary sensibilities and sensitivities helped so much to hone and shape this book; to Glen Edelstein for the artistically magnificent cover; to Colin Rolfe for being the kind and caring shepherd of design, and to Ginger Price, along with Sara Sgarlat, joining with the Monkfish team for this endeavor, to tell you and the world about this book.

Achrona, achrona chavivah. The last is the most beloved. My holy wife Ellen has rightly been called, "A Modern-Day Prophet," "A Woman of Vision," and "A Connector of Worlds." She is a Channel of the Divine, a Spirit-Sister of Shechinah, and the Embodiment of Eternal Love. She is cherished by our family and friends; by her colleagues; by our congregants who adore their sweet and holy Rebbetzin; and by her thousands of clients, students, and grand-students who have embraced Soul Memory Discovery and "The Cosmic Times" for heal-ing and guidance. Ellen's influence is felt on every page of this book, especially in the chapters indicated in the Notes, where her original thinking was the catalyst for my ideation. I have humbly and proudly said it before; I happily say it again: In the words of Rabbi Akiba speaking about his wife, *She'li v'she'lachem she'lah*—"Everything I am, anything you may learn from me, is thanks to her."

And, always, always—first and forever—to the Holy One who is "my life and the length of my days," whose words and precepts guide my Be-ing, and whose vision and promise of the evolution and trans-formation of our world animate, power, and inspire my journey.

Thank You, God. Thank You, God. Thank you, God.

SOURCES

- All biblical quotations are taken from *JPS Hebrew-English Tanakh,* (Philadelphia: Jewish Publication Society, 2000), or from the author's original translation, or from a combination of both.

  Quotations from the New Testament are from *The Holy Bible: New Revised Standard Edition with Apocrypha,* (New York: Oxford University Press USA, 1989).

  The abbreviation BT is Babylonian Talmud, major compilation of Jewish law, ca. 600 CE. The cited reference is to tractate and page.

- Many of the stories in this book are culled from the oral traditions of multiple ethnic, cultural, tribal, religious, and faith communities. These legends, fables, myths, tales, and stories are remembered by the author as campfire stories or bedtime stories, or pulpit-messages coming from Elders and Guides. Such accounts offer simple, illustrative examples often characterized by their breathtaking "wow" factor for teaching deep, meaningful lessons and passing on spiritual heritage and inheritance. Archetypal stories of this genre exist in varying forms and various collections as world-wisdom.

- *zt"l* is the English abbreviation, indicating the Hebrew words, *Zecher Tzadik L'vracha,* meaning, "May the memory of the righteous be a blessing." It is used throughout to indicate that an esteemed teacher or community leader is now deceased. His/

her teachings are still so profound that they continue to be quoted for their wisdom.

⪧ There are four modern-master spiritual World Wisdom Teachers whose wisdom is oft-quoted in this book. Here are their brief biographies:

ELIE WIESEL *zt"l*
(1928–2016) Holocaust survivor, prolific author, political activist, founding Chair of the United States Holocaust Memorial, global social conscience, 1986 Nobel Peace Prize Laureate.

RABBI SHLOMO CARLEBACH *zt"l*
(1925–1994) German-born American rabbi and musician—who with his family escaped from the Holocaust—known as "The Singing Rabbi" and as "Reb Shlomo," whose more than four thousand musical compositions based on Bible and liturgy—and tireless travel, singing, and teaching—endeared him to generations of young people whom he called his "holy hippies." These devoted followers credit him with bringing them back to Jewish spiritual life.

RABBI DR. ABRAHAM JOSHUA HESCHEL *zt"l*
(1907–1972) Polish born, German-educated American rabbi, scholar, spiritual mystic, prolific author, and political activist in Civil Rights and Antiwar movements; professor at the Hebrew Union College, Cincinnati, and the Jewish Theological Seminary, New York.

RABBI ZALMAN SCHACHTER-SHALOMI *zt"l*
(1924–2014) Polish born, Austrian-reared Holocaust refugee, American rabbi, known as Reb Zalman—brilliant, creative scholar and liturgist; inspiring teacher, author, deep ecumenist, founder and "grandfather" of the Jewish Renewal movement credited with reviving "Spiritual Judaism" in a rational age.

NOTES

OF THEN AND NOW

1. Japanese legend sourced in the existence of hundreds of "Tsunami Stones" (some centuries old) dotting the coast of Japan, carved with warnings to future generations that earthquake(s) followed by tsunami(s) had taken place at the location of the stone, admonishing others not to build houses or plant fields below certain heights.

ON THIS JOURNEY

1. Desiderius Erasmus Roterodamus (1466–1536), Dutch Catholic priest and theologian; made popular by the Swiss psychiatrist, Carl Gustav Jung (1875–1961) on a plaque that hung in his doorway.

2. United States Attorney General, New York Senator, and presidential candidate, Robert F. Kennedy (1925–1968) paraphrasing George Bernard Shaw in various speeches, and recorded in *Robert Kennedy in His Own Words: The Unpublished Recollections of the Kennedy Years* (New York: Bantam, 1989).

IN THE VERY, VERY BEGINNING

1. Gen. 1:1ff. biblical account of creation summarized.

THEN WHAT HAPPENED?

1. Gen. 2:16–17, 3:6, 3:22–23.

2. The language of the Shechinah story, and the concept of Herstory: Ellen Kaufman Dosick.

DEAR ONES

1. Based on the report issued by the National Institute of Health/Human Genome Research Institute, March 2006.

2. Edward Nydle (1954–) in a public posting on Facebook, November 1, 2017.

ENTERING THE WORLD OF SPIRIT

1. These two stories are told in slightly different form in: Rabbi Wayne Dosick, *Soul Judaism: Dancing with God into a New Era,* (Woodstock, VT: Jewish Lights, 1999).

BEING IN THE WORLD OF SPIRIT

1. Teaching of Rabbi Shlomo Carlebach *zt"l* that the biblical phrase "Face to Face" means that God and human beings know each other from the very depths of their beings.

BUT I DON'T BELIEVE

1. The scientific explanation of the "Big Bang Theory," first articulated in 1927 by Belgian Catholic priest Georges Lemaitre (1894–1966), that the universe was created approximately 13.8 billion years ago with a small singularity that inflated and expanded. Beginning in 2007, the phrase made its way into popular culture as the name of a long-running American television program produced by CBS.

2. Based on an old Mesopotamian tale retold in BT Sukkah 53b, and retold in numerous languages and settings throughout the centuries.

3. Elie Wiesel *zt"l* in his Nobel Peace Prize acceptance speech on December 10, 1986 (Oslo, Norway).

4. Attributed to Edmund Burke, Anglo-Irish philosopher (1729–1797).

BUT WE ARE AFRAID

1. Chasidic Rabbi Nachman of Bratlsav (a.k.a. Breslov) (1772–1810), *Likutey Moharan* 248.

ALL IS LOVE—LOVE IS ALL

1. Matt. 5:4; Lev. 19:3; I John 4:7; Lev. 19:7.

2. Attributed to Rabbi Jules Harlow (1931–).

3. Attributed to Chasidic Rabbi Simcha Bunim of Peshischa (Poland) (ca. 1765–1827).

4. Attributed to a story (in a number of different forms) told about Israel ben Eliezer, the Baal Shem Tov (1700–1760), founder of the Chasidic movement who was known as a mystic healer and "miracle worker."

BEING HOLY

1. Based on Deut. 29:9 and Sh'mot Rabbah 26:6.

2. Ex. 19:13; Ex. 22:26; Ex. 21:18; Lev. 19:35; Deut. 20:10; based on Ex. 23:1 and Prov. 10:1.

SKY BLUE

1. Rabbi Dr. Chaim Potok *zt"l* (1929–2002), *The Gift of Asher Lev* (New York: Knopf, 1990).

2. Rabbi Dr. Abraham Joshua Heschel *zt"l*, *Man Is Not Alone* (New York: Macmillan, 1951).

3. From the recording of *Hu Elokeinu* on the audio tape, *U'vene Yerushalayim*.

4. Yochanan ben Zakkai in Avot D'Rabbi Natan 31b.

5. Alan Alda (1936–) American Emmy-winning actor and screenwriter/

director, in a graduation speech for Connecticut College, New London, CT, June 1, 1980.

THE DAY IS DAWNING

1. Age-old scientific cosmological theory, currently termed "Precession of the Equinoxes—from Darkness to Light."
2. Jesuit priest, Fr. Pierre Teilhard de Chardin (1881–1955) in *The Phenomenon of Man* (Paris: William Collins, 1955).
3. Rabbi Shlomo Carlebach *zt"l*, on many recordings and sung at many performances throughout the world.

KNOWING BEYOND KNOWING

1. "Holy sparks" (*Ni'tza'tzot K'do'shot*), an idiom for the Presence of God within us based on the teachings of the Kabbalistic master, Isaac Luria (a.k.a. the Ari) (1534–1572) and enhanced by the teachings of the Chasidic master, the Baal Shem Tov.

INNER JOURNEYS

1. Aldous Huxley, *The Perennial Philosophy* (New York: Harper & Row, 1944).
2. The Kotzker Rebbe, Chasidic Rabbi Menachem Mendel of Kotzk *zt"l* (1787–1859).
3. From Kabbalistic and Chasidic prayer modes:
    "Do Not Fear"—*Al tirah*
    "Spiritual Intent"—*Kavannah*
    "Silence"—*Sh'tikah*
    "Merge and Flow"—*D'vekut*
    "Isolation"—*Hitbodedut*
    "Self-Understanding"—*Hitbonenut*
    "Be in Ecstasy"—*Hitlahavut*
    "Listen"—*Sh'ma.*
4. Martin Buber (1878–1965), Austrian-born, Israeli-Jewish philosopher. The title of his book, *I And Thou,* originally published in German in 1923 as *Ich und Du* (first English translation, New York: Charles Scribner's and Sons, 1937).
5. Ps. 46:1; inspired by Rabbi Peter Knobel *zt"l* (1943–2019); various biblical passages, including responses to God's call from Abraham, Jacob, and Moses; Jewish liturgy; Father James J. O'Leary, S. J. (1932–).

LINEAGE AND LEGACY

I am grateful to my wife, Ellen Kaufman Dosick, for her foundational guidance in formulating these ideas:

1. For a complete discussion of these ideas, see Rabbi Tirzah Firestone, PhD, *Wounds into Wisdom: Healing Intergenerational Jewish Trauma* (Rhinebeck, NY: Adam Kadmon Books/Monkfish Publishing, 2019).
2. From the teachings of Norman Cousins (1915–1990) in *Anatomy of an*

Illness as Perceived by the Patient (New York: Bantam, 1985); Emoto Masaru (1943–2014) in *The Hidden Messages in Water* (New York: Atria Books/Simon & Schuster, 2005); and Larry Dossey, MD (1940–) in *Healing Words: The Power of Prayer and the Practice of Medicine* (San Francisco: HarperSanFrancisco, 1995).

BEING IN AWE
1. BT Berachot, 33b.

BEING IN GRATITUDE AND JOY
1. Ruth Brin (1921–2009), American poet. Prayer "For the Blessing" from *Harvest: Collected Poems and Prayers* (New York: Reconstructionist Press, 1986).
2. Attributed to Johann Wolfgang von Goethe (1749–1832), German writer and statesman.
3. Attributed to Marcus Aurelius (121–180 CE), Roman Emperor (161–180 CE).
4. Attributed to Blessed Columba Marmion, born Joseph Aloysius Marmion (1858–1923), Irish Catholic Benedictine monk beatified September 3, 2000.

BEING IN THE GARDEN
1. Attributed to Rabbi Shimon bar Yochai, second-century sage (d. 160 CE), Midrash Rabbah, Vayikra 4:6.
2. Excerpt from *Earth Prayers from Around the World* (for the United Nations Environmental Sabbath Program), eds. Elizabeth Roberts and Elias Amidon, August 10, 2010.

BEING HUMAN
1. Ban Ki-moon (1944–), Korean diplomat, Secretary General of the United Nations (2007–2016), at International Conference of the UN's LGBTQ Core Group, Path2Equality, September 21, 2016.

BRAIDING
1. Title of a book by John Gray, PhD (New York: Harper Collins, 1994) and title of a book by Carol Gilligan (Cambridge, MA: Harvard University Press, 1982).
2. A core teaching of Carl Gustav Jung (1875–1961), Swiss psychiatrist, founder of analytical psychology.
3. Rabbi Wayne Dosick, inspired by Ellen Kaufman Dosick, Rabbi Diane Elliot, Rabbi Leah Novick, and Joan Ellen Thomas; sourced in the image of the Tree in Gen. 2:9, reflected in the Jewish liturgical "Prayer Returning the Torah to the Ark" with the addition of Lam. 5:2.

TEACH YOUR CHILDREN WELL
1. These children are known as the "Indigo Children." For a full description and explanation, see: Wayne Dosick and Ellen Kaufman Dosick, *Empowering Your Indigo Child* (San Francisco: Weiser, 2009); originally published as *Spiritually Healing the Indigo Children* (San Diego: Jodere, 2004).

RE-FRAMING

1. Alternately attributed to Irish poet William Butler Yeats (1865–1939); British philosopher, political activist and Nobel Laureate in Literature Bertrand Russell (1872–1970); or (most likely) British author and poet Eden Phillpotts (1862–1960) in *A Shadow Passes* (England: 1918).

CREATING SACRED COMMUNITY

1. Barbara Myerhoff (1935–1985), *Number Our Days* (New York: Touchstone Books/Simon and Schuster, 1980).
2. William J. (Bill) Clinton (1946–), President of the United States 1993–2001 at the dedication of his Presidential Library, Little Rock, AR, November 18, 2004.

THE POWER OF ONE

1. Concept articulated by John Naisbitt (1929–), Nana Naisbitt, and Douglas Phillips, *High Teach, High Touch: Technology and Our Search for Meaning* (New York: Broadway/Crown, 1999), based on a chapter in John Naisbitt's *Megatrends: Ten New Directions for Transforming Our Lives* (New York: Warner Books, 1982).
2. Rabbi Tanchum ben Chanilani, a third-century teacher (probably returned from Babylonia to ancient Palestine), in Eccles. Rabbah 7:30. I tell this family story in my books, *The Business Bible* (New York: William Morrow, 1993) and *Golden Rules* (San Francisco: HarperSanFancisco, 1995).
3. President John F. Kennedy, Commencement Address for American University, Washington DC, June 10, 1963—now widely quoted.
4. Rabbi Dr. Abraham Joshua Heschel *zt"l* in *The Sabbath (FSG Classics),* (New York: Farrar, Straus & Giroux, 1951).

THE POWER OF ALL

1. Attributed to Oliver Wendell Holmes Jr. (1841–1935), Justice and Acting Chief Justice of the US Supreme Court—1902-1932.
2. District of Columbia v. Heller, 2008.

THE ETERNAL SOUL

1. Attributed to the Rabbi Israel Meir Kagan *zt"l* (1839–1933), scholar, ethicist, and yeshiva founder and head in Belarus and Poland; known by the name of his 1873 book, *Chofetz Chaim* (Desirer of Life), famous for its instruction about the laws of gossip and slander.
2. The Kotzker Rebbe, Chasidic Rabbi Menachem Mendel of Kotzk *zt"l* (1787–1859).
3. Attributed to Theodore Roethke (1908–1963), American poet, in "Infirmity."
4. *Union Prayer Book I* (Cincinnati: Central Conference of American Rabbis, 1940).
5. Ps. 128:2 and Pirkae Avot 4:1. I am grateful to my teacher, mentor, and

friend, Rabbi Dr. Yehuda Shabatay (1929–), for impressing this teaching on me.

RIGHT NOW

1. Ellen Kaufman Dosick, *Soul Memory Discovery, Cosmic Times: Spiritual News You Can Use*, vol. 84, October 2017, www.soulmemorydiscovery.com.

2. Concept and terminology developed by Rabbi David Cooper *zt"l* in *God Is a Verb: Kabbalah and the Practice of Mystical Judaism* (New York: Riverhead Books, 1997).

3. I am in deep gratitude to my holy wife, spiritual sage, and modern-day prophet, Ellen Kaufman Dosick, for the concept, inspiration, and imagery of this, a capstone chapter of this book.

WHO ARE WE?

1. Rabbi Dr. Eugene Mihaly *zt"l* (1918–2002) in the Inauguration Service for Rabbi Dr. Alfred Gottschalk *zt"l* (1930–2009) as President of the Hebrew Union College–Jewish Institute of Religion, Cincinnati, OH, February 24, 1972.

BIRTHING OUR NEW WORLD

1. Ellen Kaufman Dosick, "The Soul Memory Discovery Advanced Workshop 2017: Ease and Grace."

YES ... AND: A PERSONAL WORD

1. Adaptation from Santayana attributed to Spanish philosopher and poet Jorge Agustín Nicolás Ruiz de Santayana y Borrás, a.k.a. George Santayana (1863–1952).

AND WE ALL SAY

1. US Senator from Massachusetts, Edward M. (Ted) Kennedy (1932–2009), at the Democratic National Convention, New York, August 12, 1980.

ABOUT THE AUTHOR

RABBI WAYNE DOSICK, PhD, DD, is an educator, writer, and spiritual guide who teaches and counsels about faith, ethical values, life transformations, and evolving human consciousness.

Well-known for his quality scholarship and sacred spirit, he is the rabbi of The Elijah Minyan, a retired visiting professor at the University of San Diego, and the host of the monthly Internet radio program, *SpiritTalk Live!* heard on HealthyLife.net.

He is the best-selling award-winning author of nine critically acclaimed books, including the now-classic *Living Judaism*, *Golden Rules*, *The Business Bible*, *When Life Hurts*, *20 Minute Kabbalah*, *Soul Judaism*, *The Best is Yet To Be*, *Empowering Your Indigo Child*, and, most recently, *The Real Name of God: Embracing the Full Essence of the Divine.*

Articles about Dr. Dosick have appeared in scores of newspapers and periodicals, and he is a frequent interview guest on radio and television. He is a popular speaker, who teaches, and conducts seminars throughout the country.

He has been called a "rational intellect with the soul of a mystic, a "prophet for modern times," a "gentle master of the human heart," and has been proclaimed "a spiritual master of our time."

Rabbi Dosick lives in north suburban San Diego, with his wife, Ellen Kaufman Dosick, MSW, where their home is a center of prayer, learning, and healing, and is a gathering place for spiritual seekers.

For more information about

Radical Loving,

Awesome Holiness

and the

Radical Loving Spirit Quests

please visit the website

RadicalLovingBook.com